DEBATE Pro
Book 3

DARAKWON

Author Jonathan S. McClelland
- BA in English with a Writing Concentration, University of South Carolina, Columbia, SC, USA
- Former English instructor at Daewon Foreign Language High School
- Current debate instructor for elementary school students
- Former curriculum developer at Korean Army Intelligence School
- Expert test developer of TOEFL, TOEIC, and TEPS

DEBATE Pro Book 3

Publisher Chung Kyudo
Editors Hong Inpyo, Cho Sangik
Proofreader Michael A. Putlack
Designers Zo Hwayoun, Choi Jungeun

First Published in October 2013
By Darakwon, Inc.
Darakwon Bldg., 211, Munbal-ro, Paju-si, Gyeonggi-do 10881
Republic of Korea
Tel: 82-2-736-2031 (Ext. 250)
Fax: 82-2-732-2037

Copyright © 2013 Darakwon, Inc.

All rights reserved. No part of this publication may be reproduced, stored in a retrieval system, or transmitted in any form or by any means, electronic, mechanical, photocopying or otherwise, without the prior consent of the copyright owner. Refund after purchase is possible only according to the company regulations. Contact the above telephone number for any inquiries. Consumer damages caused by loss, damage, etc. can be compensated according to the consumer dispute resolution standards anndounced by the Korea Fair Trade Commission. An incorrectly collated book will be exchanged.

ISBN 978-89-277-0687-8 58740
978-89-277-0677-9 58740 (set)

www.darakwon.co.kr

Components Main Book / Workbook
15 14 13 12 11 10 9   25 26 27 28 29

Instilling Knowledge and Skills
for Thoughtful Debate

DEBATE Pro

Book 3

DARAKWON

Preface

The *Debate Pro* series is designed to provide students with an intermediate EFL ability with a sound understanding of a variety of debate topics and develop their speaking, listening, and critical thinking skills through debate. The series consists of eight sets of books, each of which includes a Main Book and a Workbook. Each Main Book includes five chapters covering five debate skills. Within each chapter, there are two units which each cover different topics for a total of ten debate topics per book. The Workbook supplements the Main Book by helping students understand the topic more deeply, developing skills for making examples and doing research, and evaluating the debates. The Workbook can be used in class and for homework assignments.

In the book, every debate topic is introduced with a large color photograph relating to the topic. Students are asked to analyze the picture and formulate opinions about the topic through a series of six warm-up questions. The topic is then explained in more detail through a reading passage of about 300 words which briefly presents background information about the topic before outlining arguments in favor of and against the topic. The passages are followed by vocabulary and comprehension exercises. Students are then required to apply what they have learned from the passage to answer a series of in-depth questions relating to the debate topic. Following these questions, students are given opinion examples before learning the debate skill for each topic. Finally, students will have the chance to apply their knowledge to create a full debate with the assistance of sample arguments and a debate flow chart.

Each book provides free MP3 files with recordings of the reading passages and opinion examples for every unit. There is also a Teacher's Guide available at www.darakwon.co.kr that includes answer keys and sample answers for every unit as well as teaching tips and suggestions for supplementing the material.

The *Debate Pro* series has the following features:

- Ten different debate topics per book covering a range of themes including education, technology, relationships, and responsibility
- Reading passages which provide a general understanding of arguments both for and against the given topic
- Questions that require students to formulate arguments and supporting opinions about each topic
- Five different debate skills per book designed to improve students' critical thinking and speaking skills
- Sample opinions and argument examples which help students develop their own arguments
- Free MP3 files with recordings of all passages and sample opinions

Contents

About This Book _7

Chapter 1
Making Comparisons in Reasons

- **Unit 01** Public Smoking Ban _12
- **Unit 02** Cell Phones for Children _22

Chapter 2
Explaining Cause and Effect in Reasons

- **Unit 03** Hosting the Olympics _34
- **Unit 04** Alternative Energy _44

Chapter 3
Explaining Processes in Reasons

- **Unit 05** Standardized Tests _56
- **Unit 06** Human Cloning _66

Chapter 4
Creating Personal Experience Examples

- **Unit 07** Immigration _78
- **Unit 08** Advertising Directed at Children _88

Chapter 5
Creating Factual Examples

- **Unit 09** Free College Education _100
- **Unit 10** Mandatory Military Service _110

About This Book

Overview

Debate Pro main book consists of five chapters. Each chapter contains two units with each focusing on the same debate skill. Every unit is further subdivided into part A and part B. Part A, Learning about the Topic, introduces students to the topic of the unit and consists of approximately one hour of learning material. Part B, Debating the Topic, requires students to formulate their arguments and debate the topic of the unit. The total time required for Part B is also approximately one hour.

Introduction for each section

Warm-up

This part includes a picture related to the topic for students to analyze. The pictures are followed by six warm-up questions. The questions in Part A require students to analyze the picture and can be answered as a class. In Part B, students draw upon their knowledge about the topic to answer questions with a partner.

Reading Passage

This part consists of a single reading passage approximately 300 words in length. The passage introduces general background information about the topic and presents specific arguments with examples both in favor of and against the topic.

Vocabulary Check

Each reading passage is followed by five vocabulary questions to bolster students' vocabulary and ensure their understanding of the passage.

Comprehension Questions

Each reading passage includes four paired-choice reading comprehension questions. The questions ask students about the main idea of passage, factual information, and reasoning from the passage.

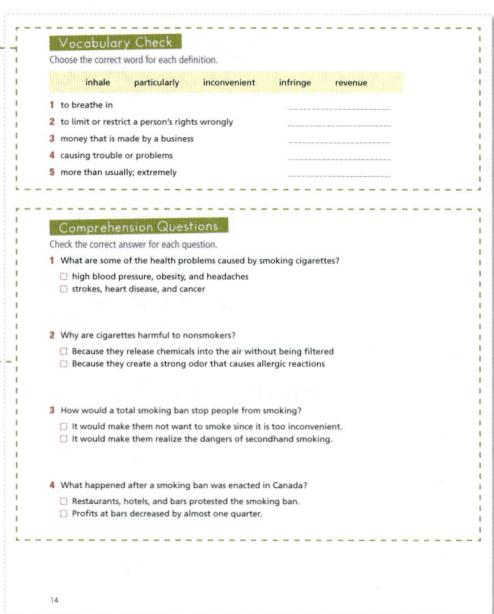

Questions for Debate

This portion consists of five open-ended questions related to the topic. The students must formulate opinions about each question and give reasons for their opinions. Key phrases are provided to help students improve their speaking skills.

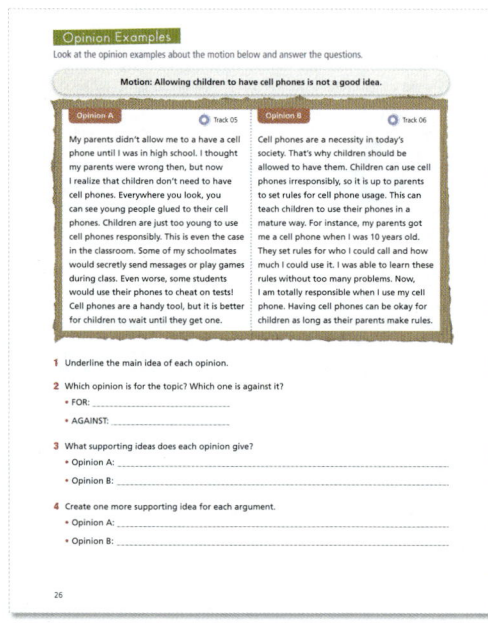

Opinion Examples

In this section, two opinion examples for and against the topic are provided. Students are required to understand the main idea of each example opinion and its supporting arguments. They must also provide an additional argument for each opinion.

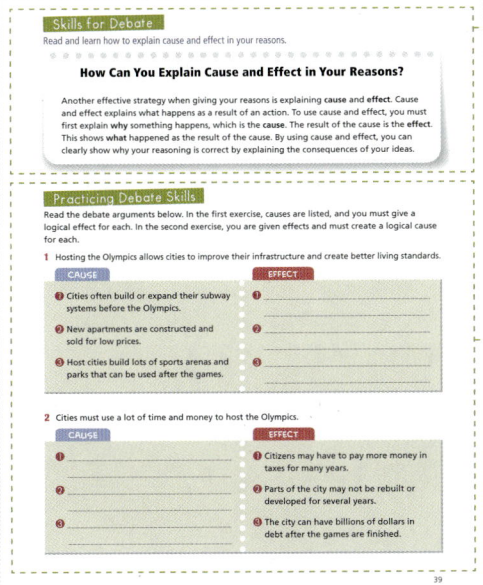

Skills for Debate

This section introduces a debate skill and explains key concepts related to the topic. Each chapter focuses on a single debate skill across two units.

Practicing Debate Skills

This exercise follows each debate skill explanation to ensure that students understand the skill and can use it during their debate.

Creating Your Debate

This section begins by introducing the skills of ARE: Argument, Reason, and Example. Following this are two sample arguments, one for PRO and one for CON, with sample notes for the ARE. On the next page are three blank columns for students to work in teams and create their AREs.

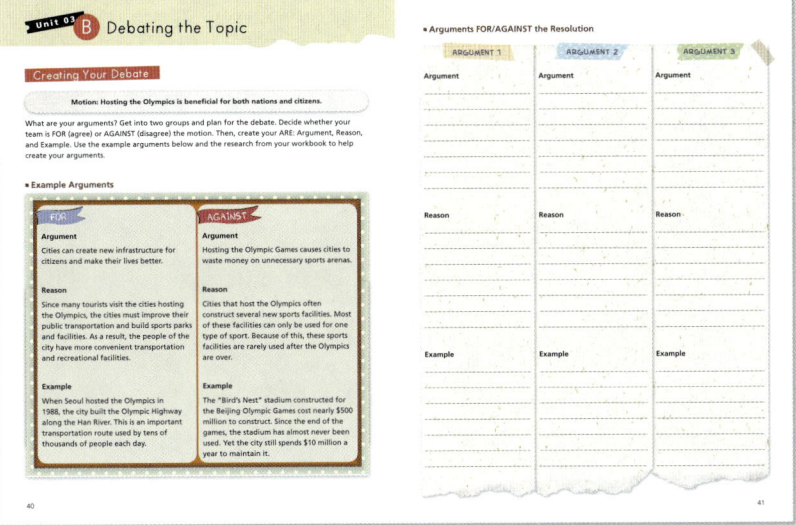

Actual Debate

This portion consists of a debate flow chart. The chart outlines the order of debate and provides sample phrases to help students use proper debate language.

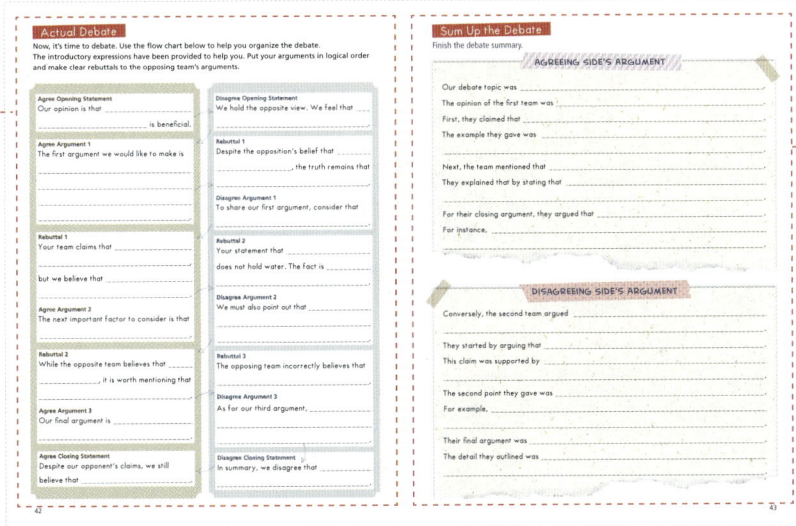

Sum Up the Debate

The final section requires students to summarize the arguments presented by both the PRO and CON teams during the debate. Sample phrases are given to help students.

Chapter 1

Making Comparisons in Reasons

Unit 01 Public Smoking Ban

Unit 02 Cell Phones for Children

Unit 01 Public Smoking Ban

WARM-UP

A. Discuss the following questions as a class.
1. What do you see in the picture above?
2. What does the sign instruct people to do?
3. Why do you think smoking is not allowed in the area in the photograph?

B. Answer the following questions with a partner.
1. Does anyone in your family smoke? If so, how often does that person smoke?
2. How can smoking in public places affect other people?
3. Do you think governments have the right to ban people from smoking in public?

Unit 01 A Learning about the Topic

Should people be allowed to smoke in public?

Read the passage and underline the main ideas.  Track 01

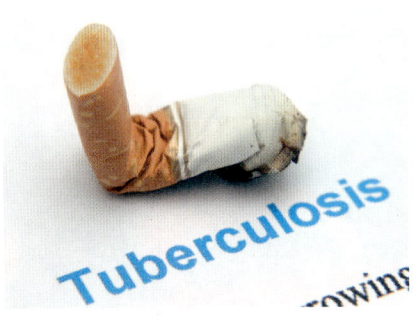

There is little debate over whether smoking cigarettes is harmful to the body. Hundreds of studies have shown that smoking can cause cancer, strokes, and heart disease. While the dangers of smoking are clear, it is far less clear whether people should have the right to smoke in public. Should people be allowed to light up in public places?

Most of the arguments in favor of a public smoking ban are medical. When people smoke, lots of smoke is produced. When nonsmokers **inhale** this smoke, it is called secondhand smoke. Secondhand smoke is **particularly** dangerous because all of the chemicals from the cigarette are released into the air unfiltered. Studies have found that people who live with smokers have a 20 to 30 percent greater chance of developing lung cancer than people who do not. Some have suggested a partial smoking ban. This is where restaurants and cafés have separate smoking areas. The problem with this is that workers in these businesses would still suffer the effects of secondhand smoke. To correct this, smoking must be totally banned. Supporters of a total ban believe that it would encourage smokers to give up their habit. The reasoning is that people would not want to smoke when it becomes too **inconvenient** to do so.

Not everybody believes public anti-smoking laws are a good idea. Critics say that such a ban **infringes** on people's rights. Since smoking cigarettes is legal, people should be allowed to smoke wherever they want. A related argument is that businesses, not the government, should have the right to choose whether to ban smoking. Research suggests that prohibiting public smoking would have serious economic impacts on businesses. In places where smoking is common, such as restaurants, hotels, and bars, a smoking ban could reduce profits since fewer people would visit these places. This was the case in the Canadian province Ontario after a public smoking ban was enacted. A study there found that **revenues** at bars were down nearly 25 percent following a ban on public smoking.

Vocabulary Check

Choose the correct word for each definition.

> inhale   particularly   inconvenient   infringe   revenue

1. to breathe in
2. to limit or restrict a person's rights wrongly
3. money that is made by a business
4. causing trouble or problems
5. more than usually; extremely

Comprehension Questions

Check the correct answer for each question.

1. What are some of the health problems caused by smoking cigarettes?
   - ☐ high blood pressure, obesity, and headaches
   - ☐ strokes, heart disease, and cancer

2. Why are cigarettes harmful to nonsmokers?
   - ☐ Because they release chemicals into the air without being filtered
   - ☐ Because they create a strong odor that causes allergic reactions

3. How would a total smoking ban stop people from smoking?
   - ☐ It would make them not want to smoke since it is too inconvenient.
   - ☐ It would make them realize the dangers of secondhand smoking.

4. What happened after a smoking ban was enacted in Canada?
   - ☐ Restaurants, hotels, and bars protested the smoking ban.
   - ☐ Profits at bars decreased by almost one quarter.

Questions for Debate

Think of and share ideas to explore the debatable issues in the article. Be sure to state your opinion clearly and to provide one supporting idea for each opinion.

1 Do you ever feel sick or uncomfortable when people smoke in public places?

When people smoke in public, I feel _____
_____.

This is due to the fact that _____
_____.

2 Do you believe smokers ever think about other people when they smoke in public?

My feeling is _____
_____.

More specifically, _____
_____.

3 Can a public smoking ban actually be effective? Why or why not?

I feel that _____
_____.

For example, _____
_____.

4 What do you think an appropriate punishment for someone caught smoking in public?

My belief is _____
_____.

To clarify, _____
_____.

5 Is it the government's responsibility to control people's unhealthy habits? Explain.

From my point of view, it is obvious that _____
_____.

Think about how _____
_____.

Opinion Examples

Look at the opinion examples about the motion below and answer the questions.

Motion: Smoking in public areas should be banned by the government.

Opinion A
 Track 02

I think that smoking cigarettes is a bad habit. However, it shouldn't be up to the government to decide where people can and cannot smoke. We live in a free society. This means that businesses and individuals alike have the legal right to make their own decisions. Second, there are already plenty of places where nonsmokers can avoid secondhand smoke. Many people enjoy going to restaurants and bars because they can smoke there. People who don't smoke can choose to visit businesses that ban smoking. Overall, this issue comes down to personal freedom. If the government bans public smoking, then our freedom is being taken away.

Opinion B
 Track 03

The government makes laws to protect citizens. Smoking is a harmful activity and must not be allowed in public places. I completely agree that adults who want to smoke should have the right to do so. The problem is that when people smoke in public places, other people are affected. Secondhand smoke presents a serious health risk. Studies show that secondhand smoking is actually more dangerous than smoking cigarettes directly. By allowing public smoking, nonsmokers suffer against their will. Governments already restrict other unhealthy behavior, such as drinking alcohol in public. Why should cigarettes be treated any differently?

1. Underline the main idea of each opinion.

2. Which opinion is for the topic? Which one is against it?
   - FOR: _____
   - AGAINST: _____

3. What supporting ideas does each opinion give?
   - Opinion A: _____
   - Opinion B: _____

4. Create one more supporting idea for each argument.
   - Opinion A: _____
   - Opinion B: _____

Skills for Debate

Read and learn how to make comparisons in your reasons.

How Can You Make Comparisons in Your Reasons?

When explaining your supporting reasons, a good strategy is **making comparisons** between your argument and ones that are similar to it. Comparisons show how the arguments about other situations can be applied to your own argument. You can compare situations that create **similar problems** or **benefits** as your argument. You can also think of situations where a **similar solution** to your situation can work. To make your comparison clearer, use **comparison words** and **phrases**. These include "like," "as," "similar to," or "such as." Making comparisons is an excellent way to strengthen your arguments.

Practicing Debate Skills

Read each of the debate arguments below and their supporting reasons. Then, think of a comparison to strengthen your supporting reasons. Finally, underline the comparison words and phrases that you use. An example is given for you.

1 Argument: Smoking creates health problems for nonsmokers.

   Reasons: Smoking creates secondhand smoke. This releases a lot of poisonous chemicals into the air. This smoke can easily make other people sick as the air is not filtered by the cigarette.

   Comparison: The situation with cigarettes is <u>similar to</u> the situation with automobiles. Some cities do not allow people to drive in the city center because the pollution can make other people sick.

2 Argument: Governments have a right to regulate smoking because it is dangerous.

   Reasons: The government creates laws to protect its citizens from harm. They want their people to be healthy and contribute to the nation. Anti-smoking laws are for the good of the people.

   Comparison: _____

3 Argument: Prohibiting smoking in public takes away people's rights.

   Reasons: In most nations, people are given the right to do what they want as long as they do not seriously harm other people. Smoking is not a serious threat to other people. Therefore, people should be allowed to smoke in public.

   Comparison: _____

Unit 01 B Debating the Topic

Creating Your Debate

Motion: Smoking in public areas should be banned by the government.

What are your arguments? Get into two groups and plan for the debate. Decide whether your team is FOR (agree) or AGAINST (disagree) the motion. Then, create your ARE: Argument, Reason, and Example. Use the example arguments below and the research from your workbook to help create your arguments.

■ Example Arguments

FOR

Argument

Smoking in public can create health problems for other people.

Reason

Cigarettes release chemicals as they burn. These chemicals are actually more harmful for nonsmokers than they are for the person smoking. The reason is the chemicals are not filtered as they leave the cigarette.

Example

Cigarettes contain on average 4,000 different chemicals. Around 70 of these chemicals, including tar, arsenic, and cadmium, are known to cause cancer. When people smoke cigarettes, all of these chemicals are released into the air.

AGAINST

Argument

Prohibiting smoking in public takes away personal rights.

Reason

In most societies today, people have the right to do what they want as long as they do not directly harm others. Smoking is a personal choice. The consequences of smoking most directly harm the smoker. In this case, the government has no reason to restrict a personal activity.

Example

Political writer Christopher Hitchens claimed that anti-smoking laws are not designed to protect nonsmokers but rather limit the freedom of smokers.

Arguments FOR/AGAINST the Motion

ARGUMENT 1

Argument

_____
_____
_____
_____
_____
_____

Reason

_____
_____
_____
_____
_____
_____

Example

_____
_____
_____
_____
_____
_____

ARGUMENT 2

Argument

_____
_____
_____
_____
_____
_____

Reason

_____
_____
_____
_____
_____
_____

Example

_____
_____
_____
_____
_____
_____

ARGUMENT 3

Argument

_____
_____
_____
_____
_____
_____

Reason

_____
_____
_____
_____
_____
_____

Example

_____
_____
_____
_____
_____
_____

Actual Debate

Now, it's time to debate. Use the flow chart below to help you organize the debate.
The introductory expressions have been provided to help you. Put your arguments in logical order and make clear rebuttals to the opposing team's arguments.

Agree Opening Statement
Our team feels that _____ _____ should be banned.

Disagree Opening Statement
We disagree with the notion that _____ _____ is a good idea.

Agree Argument 1
To begin with, _____ _____ _____ _____ _____.

Rebuttal 1
The agree team's opening argument is flawed because _____ _____ _____.

Disagree Argument 1
The first reason we oppose this topic is _____ _____ _____.

Rebuttal 1
It is incorrect to believe that _____ _____ because _____ _____ _____.

Rebuttal 2
Once again, the pro team wrongly argues that _____ _____ _____.

Agree Argument 2
The second point we would like to make is _____ _____.

Disagree Argument 2
Our second argument is _____ _____ _____.

Rebuttal 2
The opposition claims that _____ _____ _____.
What they fail to mention is _____ _____ _____.

Rebuttal 3
Your third argument overlooks the fact that _____ _____ _____.

Disagree Argument 3
Last, but not least, it must be said that _____ _____ _____.

Agree Argument 3
Finally, we must mention that _____ _____ _____.

Agree Closing Statement
In summation, it is clearly evident that _____ _____ _____.

Disagree Closing Statement
Our overall opinion regarding this topic is _____ _____.

Sum Up the Debate

Finish the debate summary.

AGREEING SIDE'S ARGUMENT

The topic of today's debate was _____.

The first team supported the topic. They felt that _____.

First, they claimed that _____.

For instance, _____
_____.

Their second argument was _____.

The example they gave was _____
_____.

For their final point, they explained that _____.

To be specific, _____
_____.

DISAGREEING SIDE'S ARGUMENT

In contrast, the opposing team believed that _____
_____.

For starters, they claimed that _____.

They supported this by mentioning that _____
_____.

The team also contended that _____.

To be more specific, _____
_____.

The final point was _____.

For example, _____
_____.

Unit 02 Cell Phones for Children

WARM-UP

A. Discuss the following questions as a class.
1. What do you see in the picture above?
2. What do you think the girl is doing with her phone?
3. How can the classroom environment change when students have cell phones?

B. Answer the following questions with a partner.
1. Do you have a cell phone? If so, when did you get it?
2. What do most children do with their cell phones?
3. Are there any problems that can occur when children have cell phones of their own?

Unit 02 A Learning about the Topic

Should children be allowed to have their own cell phones?

Read the passage and underline the main ideas. Track 04

12.1 years: this is the average age that children in the United States get their first cell phone. In the United Kingdom, the average age is lower. There, most children receive their first cell phone when they are just eight years old. In today's digital society, it makes a lot of sense for children to have their own cell phones. Still, many believe that children are too immature and **vulnerable** to carry their own mobile phones.

Cell phones are a great communication tool, but they can also be a **distraction**. Children are often **tempted** to use their phones in school. Instead of listening to their teacher, they would rather send messages to their friends or play games on their phones. In fact, 74 percent of children in one survey claimed that their friends are addicted to their cell phones. There is also the issue of cost. Cell phones—even ones designed for children—are expensive. They can cost several hundreds of dollars. Beyond that, there are the monthly phone bills that parents have to pay. Parents could save lots of money by not giving cell phones to their children. Cell phones can even introduce extra problems into children's lives. One such problem is cyber-bullying. This happens when children receive **threatening** text messages from school bullies.

Despite these drawbacks, the majority of parents still purchase phones for their children. The primary advantage is safety. Cell phones make it easy for children to contact their parents in the event of an emergency. In day-to-day situations, having a cell phone is also **handy** simply because of increased convenience. If parents are running late to pick their children up from school, they can simply call their children and let them know. This is better than having the children wait and wonder when their parents will come. Children can even benefit academically by having cell phones. Since most cell phones today have Internet browsers, it is easy for children to look up information. They can use online dictionaries, encyclopedias, college websites, and news sites to help them study. Thanks to cell phones, students can get better grades in school.

Vocabulary Check

Choose the correct word for each definition.

> vulnerable   distraction   tempted   threatening   handy

1 something that makes it difficult to think or to pay attention _____
2 very useful or helpful _____
3 easily hurt or harmed physically, mentally, or emotionally _____
4 causing somebody to do something that the person knows is wrong _____
5 suggesting bodily harm or injury _____

Comprehension Questions

Check the correct answer for each question.

1 How old on average are children in the United Kingdom when they get their first cell phone?
 - ☐ 12.1 years old
 - ☐ 8 years old

2 What problems can occur if children have cell phones in school?
 - ☐ They are likely to use the Internet to cheat on tests.
 - ☐ They might play games or send messages rather than listen to their teacher.

3 How are cell phones beneficial in emergency situations?
 - ☐ Because parents can call their children to tell them they are running late
 - ☐ Because children can quickly contact their parents if there is a problem

4 What resources are mentioned that can help students study? Choose TWO correct answers.
 - ☐ encyclopedias
 - ☐ personal blogs
 - ☐ news sites
 - ☐ school websites

Questions for Debate

Think of and share ideas to explore the debatable issues in the article. Be sure to state your opinion clearly and to provide one supporting idea for each opinion.

1. What do you think a good age for a child to get a cell phone is? Explain.

   I think that _____
   _____.

   My reasons for feeling this way are _____
   _____.

2. What are some reasons that children want to get cell phones?

   Some of the reasons are _____
   _____.

   To be more specific, _____
   _____.

3. What are some reasons that parents want to get cell phones for their children?

   It is my feeling that _____
   _____.

   For instance, _____
   _____.

4. Should parents place limitations on their children's cell phone usage? Why or why not?

   From my point of view, it seems that _____
   _____.

   To help you understand, consider that _____
   _____.

5. Do you think children mainly benefit from having cell phones or mainly suffer? Explain.

   My belief is _____
   _____.

   I believe this since _____
   _____.

Opinion Examples

Look at the opinion examples about the motion below and answer the questions.

Motion: Allowing children to have cell phones is not a good idea.

Opinion A Track 05

My parents didn't allow me to a have a cell phone until I was in high school. I thought my parents were wrong then, but now I realize that children don't need to have cell phones. Everywhere you look, you can see young people glued to their cell phones. Children are just too young to use cell phones responsibly. This is even the case in the classroom. Some of my schoolmates would secretly send messages or play games during class. Even worse, some students would use their phones to cheat on tests! Cell phones are a handy tool, but it is better for children to wait until they get one.

Opinion B Track 06

Cell phones are a necessity in today's society. That's why children should be allowed to have them. Children can use cell phones irresponsibly, so it is up to parents to set rules for cell phone usage. This can teach children to use their phones in a mature way. For instance, my parents got me a cell phone when I was 10 years old. They set rules for who I could call and how much I could use it. I was able to learn these rules without too many problems. Now, I am totally responsible when I use my cell phone. Having cell phones can be okay for children as long as their parents make rules.

1 Underline the main idea of each opinion.

2 Which opinion is for the topic? Which one is against it?
- FOR: _____
- AGAINST: _____

3 What supporting ideas does each opinion give?
- Opinion A: _____
- Opinion B: _____

4 Create one more supporting idea for each argument.
- Opinion A: _____
- Opinion B: _____

Skills for Debate

Read and learn how to make comparisons in your reasons.

How Can You Make Comparisons in Your Reasons?

In addition to comparing your argument to similar situations, you can also strengthen your argument by giving **contrasting reasons**. Contrasting reasons can be used to **point out flaws** in a situation that is **opposite** yours or to **explain why it is better**. When you do this, you should use **contrasting words** and **phrases** such as "in contrast," "unlike," "on the other hand," and "compare this to." By making contrasts between your arguments and the other side, you can make your argument more effective.

Practicing Debate Skills

Read the arguments below. For each argument, choose the most logical supporting reason and contrasting reason for each argument. Then, explain why you chose them.

1 Argument: Children can easily become addicted to cell phones.
- Supporting Reason: _____
- Contrasting Reason: _____

Explanation: _____

2 Argument: Cell phones can help children to do their schoolwork.
- Supporting Reason: _____
- Contrasting Reason: _____

Explanation: _____

3 Argument: Parents and children can stay connected in the case of an emergency.
- Supporting Reason: _____
- Contrasting Reason: _____

Explanation: _____

SUPPORTING REASONS

1. Children can access the Internet and look up information in seconds.
2. Cell phones allow people to contact each other instantly.
3. Cell phone games, the Internet, messaging, and other applications can distract children.

CONTRASTING REASONS

a. On the other hand, without a cell phone, none of these can take a child's attention.
b. Compare this to having to use a computer or a book to do research.
c. In contrast, children might not be able to get help without a cell phone.

Unit 02 B Debating the Topic

Creating Your Debate

Motion: Allowing children to have cell phones is not a good idea.

What are your arguments? Get into two groups and plan for the debate. Decide whether your team is FOR (agree) or AGAINST (disagree) the motion. Then, create your ARE: Argument, Reason, and Example. Use the example arguments below and the research from your workbook to help create your arguments.

■ Example Arguments

FOR

Argument

Children are too young to use cell phones responsibly.

Reason

Children lack self control. They are likely to spend too much time on their phones playing games and chatting with their friends. In contrast, children cannot be distracted if they do not have a cell phone.

Example

According to a study by the Kaiser Family Foundation, middle and high school students spend around one and a half hours a day using their cell phone. In many cases, the children use their phones instead of studying.

AGAINST

Argument

Parents can use cell phones as a tool to teach their children about self-control.

Reason

As children, people learn about the world in both good and bad ways. By having cell phones, children can learn about the benefits of having phones. They can also learn how spending too much time on phones has drawbacks.

Example

One survey by a cell phone company found that the majority of parents—around 80 percent—have specific rules about cell phone usage. They do this so that their children learn what an appropriate amount of time to spend using their phones is.

Arguments FOR/AGAINST the Motion

ARGUMENT 1

Argument

Reason

Example

ARGUMENT 2

Argument

Reason

Example

ARGUMENT 3

Argument

Reason

Example

Actual Debate

Now, it's time to debate. Use the flow chart below to help you organize the debate.
The introductory expressions have been provided to help you. Put your arguments in logical order and make clear rebuttals to the opposing team's arguments.

Agree Opening Statement
Regarding the topic _____, it is our team's belief that _____.

Disagree Opening Statement
Our team feels the opposite. Our opinion is _____.

Agree Argument 1
For starters, we feel that _____.

Rebuttal 1
Your team claims that _____. Yet _____.

Disagree Argument 1
As for our opening argument, we believe that _____.

Rebuttal 1
The con team said that _____. This argument is flawed because _____.

Agree Argument 2
Another reason we favor this motion is _____.

Rebuttal 2
Once again, the pro team has it wrong. The fact is _____.

Disagree Argument 2
Our next idea is that _____.

Rebuttal 2
Despite your belief that _____, we feel that _____.

Agree Argument 3
For our final argument, let us point out that _____.

Rebuttal 3
You said that _____. However, it is our opinion that _____.

Disagree Argument 3
Lastly, consider that _____.

Agree Closing Statement
To sum up, we contend that _____.

Disagree Closing Statement
Our overall opinion about this topic is _____.

Sum Up the Debate

Finish the debate summary.

AGREEING SIDE'S ARGUMENT

The topic of today's debate was _____.

The main belief of the pro team was _____.

To start with, they said that _____.

They supported this by explaining that _____
_____.

Second of all, they argued that _____.

More specifically, _____
_____.

Their final reason was _____.

For example, _____
_____.

DISAGREEING SIDE'S ARGUMENT

The opposing team argued that _____
_____.

Their opening argument was _____.

For instance, _____
_____.

The next point they brought up was _____.

In detail, _____
_____.

As for their third argument, they stated that _____.

They supported this by pointing out that _____
_____.

Chapter 2

Explaining Cause and Effect in Reasons

Unit 03 Hosting the Olympics
Unit 04 Alternative Energy

Unit 03 Hosting the Olympics

WARM-UP

A. Discuss the following questions as a class.
1. What do you see in the picture above?
2. Which of the flags can you recognize?
3. How many cities that have hosted the Olympics can you name? Give the years if you know them.

B. Answer the following questions with a partner.
1. Why do you think the Olympic Games were originally created?
2. How do nations that host the Olympics benefit?
3. What are some problems that can result from hosting the Olympics?

Unit 03   A   Learning about the Topic

Should nations compete to host the Olympics?

Read the passage and underline the main ideas.

 Track 07

In 1988, Seoul hosted the Summer Olympics. Olympic fever struck the Korean peninsula once again when Pyeongchang won the bid to host the 2018 Winter Olympics. This time, however, the benefits of hosting the Olympics are less clear for South Korea. Does hosting the Olympics allow cities to **showcase** themselves to the international community, or does it simply waste time and money?

One advantage of hosting the Olympics is that it serves as a way for nations to show their economic strength to other nations. This was definitely the case with the 1988 Seoul Olympics and the 2008 Olympics in Beijing. Related to this is the fact that cities use the Olympics to improve their **infrastructure**. To prepare for the 2012 Olympics, London spent nearly 25 billion dollars to make the London Underground more modern and safer. Lastly, hosting the Olympics creates a feeling of **goodwill** among the citizens of a city. Coming together and working toward a common goal such as hosting the Olympic Games unites the people of a city. One survey found that 97 percent of Parisians and 87 percent of Londoners wanted their cities to host the 2012 Olympics for this reason.

Hosting the Olympics also has **notable** drawbacks. First, it is tremendously expensive. Cities must build huge new stadiums and sports arenas for the games. After hosting the 1976 Olympics, Montreal had a debt of over one billion dollars that took three decades to pay off. Another disadvantage is that the bidding process is too long. Pyeongchang made its first bid to host the Winter Olympics in 1998. It did not win until its third bid 13 years later. While waiting for the result of the bid, cities have to **reserve** tax money and lands that may never be used for hosting the Olympics. Even if a city wins the right to host the Olympics, the cities that host the Olympics are generally very large and need little development assistance anyway.

Vocabulary Check

Choose the correct word for each definition.

| showcase | infrastructure | goodwill | notable | reserve |

1 to set aside for later use

2 to show something in an attractive or favorable way

3 a kind, helpful, or friendly attitude

4 the basic equipment needed for a country to function properly

5 unusual and worth noticing

Comprehension Questions

Check the correct answer for each question.

1 What is true about the 1988 and 2008 Olympic Games?
- ☐ The host nations used the Olympics to improve their infrastructure.
- ☐ The host nations used the Olympics to showcase their economic development.

2 Why did people from Paris and London want their cities to host the Olympic Games?
- ☐ Because hosting the Olympics unites citizens and creates feelings of goodwill
- ☐ Because hosting the Olympics brings international attention to a city

3 In what year did Pyeongchang finally win its bid to host the Winter Olympics?
- ☐ 1998
- ☐ 2011

4 What problem is caused by the long bidding process?
- ☐ Tax money and lands are set aside and may never be used.
- ☐ The cities that win Olympic bids usually do not need development assistance.

Questions for Debate

Think of and share ideas to explore the debatable issues in the article. Be sure to state your opinion clearly and to provide one supporting idea for each opinion.

1 Why do you think the Olympics have remained popular for more than 100 years?

My opinion is _____
_____.

For instance, _____
_____.

2 How do you feel about the fact that South Korea is hosting the 2018 Winter Olympics?

I feel that _____
_____.

I hold this belief because _____
_____.

3 Montreal spent 30 years paying off its debt from the 1976 Olympics. Do you think that was a good investment?

From my perspective, it seems that _____
_____.

For example, _____
_____.

4 Is it important for cities to showcase themselves to the rest of the world? Why or why not?

My feelings about this are _____
_____.

To go into more detail, _____
_____.

5 Do you believe the trend of cities spending more on each Olympic Games will continue? Explain.

I predict that _____
_____.

I feel this way since _____
_____.

Opinion Examples

Look at the opinion examples about the motion below and answer the questions.

Motion: Hosting the Olympics is beneficial for both nations and citizens.

Opinion A Track 08

Hosting the Olympics may cost lots of money, but it gives cities something that money alone cannot buy: respect. Several cities have used the Olympics to show the rest of the world how developed they are. This is what Seoul did in 1988 and Beijing did in 2008. Long after the games are over, the international community has lasting, positive impressions of the host cities. This brings more business and tourism to these places. Just as importantly, hosting the Olympics is fun. The citizens of a city all get excited before the games begin. Once they start, citizens can enjoy watching some of the best athletes in the world compete in dozens of different sporting events.

Opinion B Track 09

It seems to me that hosting the Olympics is a waste of time and money. First, think about the cost. To host the 2008 Olympics, Beijing spent over 40 billion dollars. This is a huge amount of money to spend on sports stadiums that will hardly be used after the Olympics are over. Another problem is that the bidding process is too long. Cities may spend more than a decade trying to host the Olympics. During this time, they have to reserve resources that may never be used. If a city needs more development, it should just go ahead and improve its infrastructure. This would be better than waiting to host an Olympic Games that might not ever happen.

1 Underline the main idea of each opinion.

2 Which opinion is for the topic? Which one is against it?
- FOR: _____
- AGAINST: _____

3 What supporting ideas does each opinion give?
- Opinion A: _____
- Opinion B: _____

4 Create one more supporting idea for each argument.
- Opinion A: _____
- Opinion B: _____

Skills for Debate

Read and learn how to explain cause and effect in your reasons.

How Can You Explain Cause and Effect in Your Reasons?

Another effective strategy when giving your reasons is explaining **cause** and **effect**. Cause and effect explains what happens as a result of an action. To use cause and effect, you must first explain **why** something happens, which is the **cause**. The result of the cause is the **effect**. This shows **what** happened as the result of the cause. By using cause and effect, you can clearly show why your reasoning is correct by explaining the consequences of your ideas.

Practicing Debate Skills

Read the debate arguments below. In the first exercise, causes are listed, and you must give a logical effect for each. In the second exercise, you are given effects and must create a logical cause for each.

1 Hosting the Olympics allows cities to improve their infrastructure and create better living standards.

CAUSE	EFFECT
❶ Cities often build or expand their subway systems before the Olympics.	❶ _____
❷ New apartments are constructed and sold for low prices.	❷ _____
❸ Host cities build lots of sports arenas and parks that can be used after the games.	❸ _____

2 Cities must use a lot of time and money to host the Olympics.

CAUSE	EFFECT
❶ _____	❶ Citizens may have to pay more money in taxes for many years.
❷ _____	❷ Parts of the city may not be rebuilt or developed for several years.
❸ _____	❸ The city can have billions of dollars in debt after the games are finished.

Unit 03 B Debating the Topic

Creating Your Debate

Motion: Hosting the Olympics is beneficial for both nations and citizens.

What are your arguments? Get into two groups and plan for the debate. Decide whether your team is FOR (agree) or AGAINST (disagree) the motion. Then, create your ARE: Argument, Reason, and Example. Use the example arguments below and the research from your workbook to help create your arguments.

■ Example Arguments

FOR

Argument

Cities can create new infrastructure for citizens and make their lives better.

Reason

Since many tourists visit the cities hosting the Olympics, the cities must improve their public transportation and build sports parks and facilities. As a result, the people of the city have more convenient transportation and recreational facilities.

Example

When Seoul hosted the Olympics in 1988, the city built the Olympic Highway along the Han River. This is an important transportation route used by tens of thousands of people each day.

AGAINST

Argument

Hosting the Olympic Games causes cities to waste money on unnecessary sports arenas.

Reason

Cities that host the Olympics often construct several new sports facilities. Most of these facilities can only be used for one type of sport. Because of this, these sports facilities are rarely used after the Olympics are over.

Example

The "Bird's Nest" stadium constructed for the Beijing Olympic Games cost nearly $500 million to construct. Since the end of the games, the stadium has almost never been used. Yet the city still spends $10 million a year to maintain it.

Arguments FOR/AGAINST the Motion

ARGUMENT 1

Argument
_____
_____
_____
_____
_____
_____
_____

Reason
_____
_____
_____
_____
_____
_____

Example
_____
_____
_____
_____
_____
_____

ARGUMENT 2

Argument
_____
_____
_____
_____
_____
_____
_____

Reason
_____
_____
_____
_____
_____
_____

Example
_____
_____
_____
_____
_____
_____

ARGUMENT 3

Argument
_____
_____
_____
_____
_____
_____
_____

Reason
_____
_____
_____
_____
_____
_____

Example
_____
_____
_____
_____
_____
_____

Actual Debate

Now, it's time to debate. Use the flow chart below to help you organize the debate.
The introductory expressions have been provided to help you. Put your arguments in logical order and make clear rebuttals to the opposing team's arguments.

Agree Opening Statement
Our opinion is that _____
_____ is beneficial.

Agree Argument 1
The first argument we would like to make is _____
_____
_____
_____.

Rebuttal 1
Your team claims that _____
_____,
but we believe that _____
_____.

Agree Argument 2
The next important factor to consider is that _____
_____.

Rebuttal 2
While the opposite team believes that _____
_____, it is worth mentioning that _____
_____.

Agree Argument 3
Our final argument is _____
_____
_____.

Agree Closing Statement
Despite our opponent's claims, we still believe that _____
_____.

Disagree Opening Statement
We hold the opposite view. We feel that _____
_____.

Rebuttal 1
Despite the opposition's belief that _____
_____, the truth remains that _____
_____.

Disagree Argument 1
To share our first argument, consider that _____
_____.

Rebuttal 2
Your statement that _____
does not hold water. The fact is _____
_____.

Disagree Argument 2
We must also point out that _____
_____
_____
_____.

Rebuttal 3
The opposing team incorrectly believes that _____
_____.

Disagree Argument 3
As for our third argument, _____
_____
_____
_____.

Disagree Closing Statement
In summary, we disagree that _____
_____.

Sum Up the Debate

Finish the debate summary.

AGREEING SIDE'S ARGUMENT

Our debate topic was _____.

The opinion of the first team was _____.

First, they claimed that _____.

The example they gave was _____
_____.

Next, the team mentioned that _____.

They explained that by stating that _____
_____.

For their closing argument, they argued that _____.

For instance, _____
_____.

DISAGREEING SIDE'S ARGUMENT

Conversely, the second team argued _____
_____.

They started by arguing that _____.

This claim was supported by _____
_____.

The second point they gave was _____.

For example, _____
_____.

Their final argument was _____.

The detail they outlined was _____
_____.

Unit 04 Alternative Energy

A. Discuss the following questions as a class.
1. What do you see in the picture above?
2. What are some advantages of using wind power?
3. What are some drawbacks of using wind power?

B. Answer the following questions with a partner.
1. Can you think of any problems with traditional energy sources such as oil?
2. What types of alternative energy sources can you think of?
3. Have you or anyone in your family used alternative energy sources? Why or why not?

Unit 04 A Learning about the Topic

Should alternative energy sources replace traditional ones?

Read the passage and underline the main ideas.  Track 10

Scientists estimate that by the year 2050, Earth's oil resources will nearly be **depleted**. This poses a major problem. Almost all of our energy currently comes from fossil fuels. It is for this reason that researchers have begun developing alternative energy sources. These include solar, wind, and hydroelectric power. These resources are **sustainable** and environmentally friendly. Even so, there is reason to be doubtful that these alternative energy sources can fully replace fossil fuels.

Fossil fuels are a great form of energy because they are so **convenient**. Oil can be easily transported across large distances by using oil tankers and pipes. However, transporting alternative energy sources is often difficult. Alternative energy sources can usually only be used in one area. This makes them **impractical** to use on a large scale. Oil energy is also more efficient than most alternative energy sources. Burning fossil fuels generally has an efficiency of 20 to 30 percent. Some oil power plants have even reported up to 60 percent efficiency. In contrast, solar power has an efficiency of less than 1 percent. Creating energy from fossil fuels is also cheaper than using alternative energy sources. Fossil fuels are widely available, and so is their technology. This makes them inexpensive to use.

Not all of the news is bad for alternative energy. For one, more types of alternative energy sources are being researched to meet different energy needs. One of these is ethanol, a biofuel. It could replace gasoline in powering cars and trucks. Ethanol allows engines to generate more power and is better for the environment. One study found that ethanol **emits** 52 percent fewer greenhouse gases than gasoline. Along with newer forms of alternative energy, existing forms of alternative energy are becoming cheaper and more efficient. For instance, Stanford University researchers have created a new type of solar panel. This new panel is 100 times more efficient than previous panels. Lastly, alternative energy will create new jobs. Workers will have to build new hydroelectric dams. Scientists will have to develop new fuel and types of solar panels. These will benefit the economy.

Vocabulary Check

Choose the correct word for each definition.

> depleted   sustainable   convenient   impractical   emit

1 to send something out from a source
2 able to be used without being completely used up
3 allowing you to do something easily and without trouble
4 all used up
5 not easy to use or do

Comprehension Questions

Check the correct answer for each question.

1 What do scientists predict will happen by the year 2050?
- ☐ Alternative energy sources will fully replace traditional energy sources.
- ☐ Nearly all the sources of oil will be used up.

2 Why are alternative energy sources not practical to use on a large scale?
- ☐ They can only be transported by oil tankers and pipes.
- ☐ They can only be used in a single location.

3 What is the usual efficiency of solar energy?
- ☐ Between 20 and 30 percent
- ☐ Less than 1 percent

4 What are the advantages of ethanol over traditional gasoline? Choose TWO correct answers.
- ☐ It produces more power.
- ☐ It creates less pollution.
- ☐ It is less expensive.
- ☐ It is more efficient.

Questions for Debate

Think of and share ideas to explore the debatable issues in the article. Be sure to state your opinion clearly and to provide one supporting idea for each opinion.

1 What are the main problems of traditional sources of energy?

Some of the problems include _____

_____.

For instance, _____

_____.

2 What are the main problems with alternative sources of energy?

The main problems are _____

_____.

To be more specific, _____

_____.

3 Do you think it is more important to have energy that is cheap or environmentally friendly? Explain.

I feel that _____

_____.

The reason is _____

_____.

4 Would you be willing to use alternative energy sources? Why or why not?

My belief is that I would _____

_____.

To put it another way, _____

_____.

5 What types of alternative energy (such as solar, wind, hydroelectric, biofuel) do you believe will be the most popular in the future? Explain.

My prediction is that _____

_____.

For example, _____

_____.

Opinion Examples

Look at the opinion examples about the motion below and answer the questions.

> **Motion: Alternative sources of energy cannot replace fossil fuels at this time.**

Opinion A Track 11

It would be great if alternative energy sources could replace traditional energy. They have severe limitations, though, that make this unlikely. For one, alternative energy is just too expensive. Solar panels are a major example of this. Sure, over the long run, they are cheaper. But the starting cost is too high. One panel can cost $3,000 or more. The infrastructure for alternative energy is also not developed enough. These days, electric cars are becoming more common. However, the number of charging stations is still very low. This means that if your car's batteries run out, you could be stuck on the side of the road with no way to get help.

Opinion B Track 12

Alternative energy is still not widespread, but it won't become more popular unless more people use it. As more people use alternative energy, it will become cheaper. Companies will find ways to create alternative energy more efficiently. Just recently, researchers at Stanford created a much more efficient solar panel. That's another point to keep in mind: Alternative energy will become more convenient as more people use it. For example, if millions of people drive electric cars, you can bet that companies will build thousands of charging stations. The only way for alternative energy to replace traditional sources is for people to start using them.

1 Underline the main idea of each opinion.

2 Which opinion is for the topic? Which one is against it?
- FOR: _____
- AGAINST: _____

3 What supporting ideas does each opinion give?
- Opinion A: _____
- Opinion B: _____

4 Create one more supporting idea for each argument.
- Opinion A: _____
- Opinion B: _____

Skills for Debate

Read and learn how to explain cause and effect in your reasons.

How Can You Explain Cause and Effect in Your Reasons?

When explaining cause and effect, you must make sure to clearly show the **relationship** between your cause and its effect. The easiest way to show connections between your ideas is by using **transitions** and **phrases**. These can include "if," "then," "so," "so that," "since," "because," "due to," and "as a result." Using clear transitions will make it easier for you to prove your point and to win your debate.

Practicing Debate Skills

Read the following debate topic. Match the causes in the left column with the matching effects in the right column. Then, use these ideas to create complete sentences with the given transitions.

- **Topic:** People must begin using renewable alternative energy sources as soon as possible.

CAUSE	EFFECT
Fossil fuels create air pollution.	They can be used forever.
Renewable energy sources rely on natural power.	Companies will create products that use environmentally friendly power.
The government makes laws to reduce automobile pollution levels.	People can have problems breathing.

- **Sentences:**

1. _____ (because)

2. _____ (as a result)

3. _____ (if)

Unit 04 B Debating the Topic

Creating Your Debate

> **Motion: Alternative sources of energy cannot replace fossil fuels at this time.**

What are your arguments? Get into two groups and plan for the debate. Decide whether your team is FOR (agree) or AGAINST (disagree) the motion. Then, create your ARE: Argument, Reason, and Example. Use the example arguments below and the research from your workbook to help create your arguments.

■ Example Arguments

FOR

Argument

Alternative energy sources are too expensive for most people.

Reason

Traditional energy sources are cheap because the infrastructure and technology for them are highly developed. On the other hand, alternative energy is not in widespread use yet. It is still experimental. As a result, it is expensive.

Example

Solar energy panels create energy at no cost, but the prices of the panels themselves are high. Typically, homeowners have to spend more than $5,000 for enough panels to power their homes.

AGAINST

Argument

Alternative energy sources are becoming more practical to use.

Reason

The increased popularity of alternative energy sources means that companies are investing more money into them. Therefore, products are becoming more efficient.

Example

Ethanol fuel is becoming more popular in places such as the United States. Because of this, companies are able to produce and transport it more cheaply. The price of ethanol is now up to 30 percent cheaper than the price of regular gasoline.

■ Arguments FOR/AGAINST the Motion

ARGUMENT 1

Argument

_____
_____
_____
_____
_____
_____

Reason

_____
_____
_____
_____
_____
_____

Example

_____
_____
_____
_____
_____
_____

ARGUMENT 2

Argument

_____
_____
_____
_____
_____
_____

Reason

_____
_____
_____
_____
_____
_____

Example

_____
_____
_____
_____
_____
_____

ARGUMENT 3

Argument

_____
_____
_____
_____
_____
_____

Reason

_____
_____
_____
_____
_____
_____

Example

_____
_____
_____
_____
_____
_____

Actual Debate

Now, it's time to debate. Use the flow chart below to help you organize the debate.
The introductory expressions have been provided to help you. Put your arguments in logical order and make clear rebuttals to the opposing team's arguments.

Agree Opening Statement
The members of the pro team feel that _____.

Agree Argument 1
For starters, _____.

Rebuttal 1
We completely disagree with that idea. _____.

Agree Argument 2
Another reason we favor this motion is _____.

Rebuttal 2
Once again, we cannot agree. The reason is _____.

Agree Argument 3
Our final argument is _____.

Agree Closing Statement
To summarize, _____.

Disagree Opening Statement
In contrast, our team contends that _____.

Rebuttal 1
You wrongly argue that _____. In fact, _____.

Disagree Argument 1
Our first point regarding this issue is _____.

Rebuttal 2
It is wrong to assume that _____ since _____.

Disagree Argument 2
The second point we would like to make is _____.

Rebuttal 3
Your contention that _____ is false because _____.

Disagree Argument 3
Lastly, we would like to point out that _____.

Disagree Closing Statement
Our overall opinion is that _____.

Sum Up the Debate

Finish the debate summary.

AGREEING SIDE'S ARGUMENT

The debate topic for today was _____.

The first team argued in favor of the topic by claiming that _____.

For one, they stated that _____.

This notion was supported by the fact that _____
_____.

Their second argument was _____.

For instance, _____
_____.

Finally, they reasoned that _____.

Their example was _____
_____.

DISAGREEING SIDE'S ARGUMENT

The con team argued against this point. They posited that _____
_____.

They began by claiming that _____.

They mentioned _____
_____ to support their claim.

Second, they brought up the idea that _____.

For example, _____
_____.

Their concluding argument was _____.

This was illustrated by _____
_____.

Chapter 3

Explaining Processes in Reasons

Unit 05 Standardized Tests

Unit 06 Human Cloning

Unit 05: Standardized Tests

WARM-UP

A. Discuss the following questions as a class.
1. What do you see in the picture above?
2. Why do most standardized tests use multiple-choice questions?
3. Why do you think the pencil in the picture is broken in half?

B. Answer the following questions with a partner.
1. Do you have to take standardized tests in school? If so, for what subjects do you take them?
2. For what reasons do you think schools give standardized tests to students?
3. Do you think standardized tests are a good way to measure students' abilities?

Unit 05 A Learning about the Topic

Should schools rely on standardized tests to evaluate students?

Read the passage and underline the main ideas.

Track 13

These days, standardized tests are one of the most important assessment tools used in education. Students cram to memorize thousands of facts to **master** these multiple-choice exams. In many ways, standardized tests are the best way to evaluate the millions of students in our modern education systems. Even so, some educators question the value of standardized tests by claiming they are a flawed and unfair way to measure students' academic skills.

A major shortcoming of standardized tests is that they only test a limited set of skills. Most standardized tests are multiple choice. They mainly measure memorization skills. Other skills such as critical thinking and creativity are rarely tested. Standardized testing also puts too much pressure on students to perform well. These tests can have a major **influence** on a student's academic future. For instance, most high school students in the United States must pass standardized tests called exit exams. Students who fail these tests cannot graduate even if they have a perfect grade point average. Teachers also feel the stress of standardized tests. For instance, teachers in the U.S. can receive pay cuts or lose their jobs based on their students' test scores. Because of this, many teachers simply "teach to the test." They **drill** students on test questions rather than creating interesting and informative lessons.

Despite standardized tests' drawbacks, almost every country continues to use them. One reason for this is that these tests **objectively** measure student ability. Standardized tests make it easy to compare how much students learn in different schools. With grades, such cross comparisons are more difficult. The reason is that each school has different grading standards. In addition, the quality of education can improve with standardized tests. Standardized tests provide an academic **framework** for schools to follow. This ensures that all students in the same grade receive similar instruction. Likewise, standardized testing keeps teachers responsible for their teaching. Students' test scores are printed and kept in records. Teachers who help students get high test scores are rewarded with gifts and pay bonuses in some countries. This motivates teachers always to try their best to educate students.

Vocabulary Check

Choose the correct word for each definition.

| master | influence | drill | objectively | framework |

1. to learn something completely _____
2. to teach someone by repeating a lesson over and over _____
3. the basic structure of something _____
4. the power to change or affect something _____
5. based on facts rather than feelings or opinions _____

Comprehension Questions

Check the correct answer for each question.

1. What types of skills do most standardized tests measure?
   - ☐ memorization skills
   - ☐ critical thinking and creativity

2. What must American high school students do in order to graduate from high school?
   - ☐ have a perfect grade point average
   - ☐ pass a standardized exit exam

3. Why is it difficult to compare how much students in different schools learn?
   - ☐ Because each school uses different standardized tests
   - ☐ Because each school follows different grading standards

4. What do some countries do to encourage teachers to help students get high test scores?
   - ☐ They give the teachers pay bonuses and presents.
   - ☐ They show teachers records of their students' test scores.

Questions for Debate

Think of and share ideas to explore the debatable issues in the article. Be sure to state your opinion clearly and to provide one supporting idea for each opinion.

1. Do you take standardized tests in your school? If so, what do you think they are for?

   In my school, I _____.

   The reason I say this is _____.

2. Why do you think the first standardized tests were created?

   I feel that _____.

   For instance, _____.

3. Do you feel that all students who have high standardized test scores are the best students? Explain.

   From my perspective, it seems that _____.

   To go into detail, _____.

4. How can standardized tests be unfair for measuring the academic performance of some students?

   It is my belief that _____.

   One example is _____.

5. Instead of using standardized tests, what are some alternatives that schools can use to measure student performance?

   My opinion is _____.

   The reason I believe this is _____.

Opinion Examples

Look at the opinion examples about the motion below and answer the questions.

Motion: Standardized tests are the most effective way to evaluate students.

Opinion A Track 14

The first standardized test was created by Harvard University to measure student ability fairly. Since then, the purpose of standardized tests hasn't changed. Schools must continue to use standardized tests. One reason is that all students are equal with standardized tests. Since all students take the same test, it's easy to compare student achievement. A student who scores a 90 on a math test is a better student than one who scores a 75. Standardized tests also help schools and teachers save time. Teachers can easily create lessons that prepare students for the tests. And since the tests are usually multiple choice, they can be graded quickly and objectively.

Opinion B Track 15

Standardized tests have been around for a long time, but that doesn't mean we should keep using them. The most obvious problem is that the tests are multiple choice. In the real world, solving a problem does not mean having four choices and choosing the best option. It means thinking critically and creatively to find the best solution. However, these skills are not measured on these tests. So it's not surprising that standardized tests don't cover what students study in class. Research by Michigan State University found that between 50 to 80 percent of the material on standardized tests is not presented in classroom instruction.

1. Underline the main idea of each opinion.

2. Which opinion is for the topic? Which one is against it?
   - FOR: _____
   - AGAINST: _____

3. What supporting ideas does each opinion give?
   - Opinion A: _____
   - Opinion B: _____

4. Create one more supporting idea for each argument.
   - Opinion A: _____
   - Opinion B: _____

Skills for Debate

Read and learn how to explain a process in your reasons.

How Can You Explain a Process in Your Reasons?

When making your reasons, you can also explain your arguments in terms of a **process**. To explain a process, you present your ideas in **the order that they happen**. This is similar to telling a story. Begin with the situation that happens first, move to the second step, and continue until you reach your **conclusion**. Using **transition words** will make your process clearer. These include **transitions of time** such as "first," "to begin with," "initially," "second," "next," "in addition," and "third." To finish your reasoning, use **concluding transitions** such as "consequently," "the result of this is," and "this leads to."

Practicing Debate Skills

Read each of the arguments below and examine their reasons. Decide the correct order of the reasons and write an appropriate transition for each. Some answers have been provided to help you.

1 Argument: Student performance can be measured objectively with standardized tests.

Reasons: _____, students' scores are determined only by their ability, not other factors.

For starters, all students are given the same questions on a standardized test.

_____, students have the same amount of time to finish their tests.

2 Argument: Standardized tests do not fairly measure the abilities of students from poorer families.

Reasons: _As a result_, poorer students often get low scores that do not show their true abilities.

_____, these students do not learn the concepts that appear on standardized tests.

_____, students from poorer families usually go to worse schools.

3 Argument: Standardized tests save schools time and money.

Reasons: _____, students fill out their answers on a multiple-choice answer sheet.

_____, schools do not have to pay teachers money to spend hours grading exams.

Second, each test can be graded in just a few seconds or less.

Unit 05 B Debating the Topic

Creating Your Debate

Motion: Standardized tests are the most effective way to evaluate students.

What are your arguments? Get into two groups and plan for the debate. Decide whether your team is FOR (agree) or AGAINST (disagree) the motion. Then, create your ARE: Argument, Reason, and Example. Use the example arguments below and the research from your workbook to help create your arguments.

- **Example Arguments**

FOR

Argument

Standardized tests make it easy for schools to measure student performance objectively.

Reason

For starters, students are all given the same test. The questions and format of the test are the same for all students. They also have the same amount of time and conditions in which to take the test. As a result, students' scores are completely the result of their ability.

Example

The SAT in the United States and the KSAT in South Korea are standardized tests used for college admissions. Every student has the same opportunity to get a good score on these tests, which is why colleges use them.

AGAINST

Argument

Standardized tests mainly test memorization, not other skills.

Reason

Most standardized tests are multiple choice. To do well, students must memorize hundreds of facts. There is no chance for students to use their creativity and to solve the problems themselves. In this way, standardized tests are very limited in the skills they measure.

Example

In the real world, there is rarely a single correct answer. Solving problems such as world hunger and global warming requires creativity and critical thinking. These skills are more important than pure memorization.

■ Arguments FOR/AGAINST the Motion

ARGUMENT 1	ARGUMENT 2	ARGUMENT 3
Argument	**Argument**	**Argument**
Reason	**Reason**	**Reason**
Example	**Example**	**Example**

Actual Debate

Now, it's time to debate. Use the flow chart below to help you organize the debate. The introductory expressions have been provided to help you. Put your arguments in logical order and make clear rebuttals to the opposing team's arguments.

Agree Opening Statement
Our team is convinced that _____
_____.

Agree Argument 1
For our first argument, we must point out that _____
_____
_____
_____.

Rebuttal 1
From our point of view, this idea is wrong. Instead, _____
_____.

Agree Argument 2
Second of all, _____
_____.

Rebuttal 2
Once again, the con team has it wrong. The fact is _____
_____.

Agree Argument 3
The final point we will mention is _____
_____
_____.

Agree Closing Statement
It is the pro team's opinion that _____
_____.

Disagree Opening Statement
We are skeptical that _____
_____.

Rebuttal 1
Our opponents claim that _____
_____.
This is flawed because _____
_____.

Disagree Argument 1
As for our first argument, _____
_____.

Rebuttal 2
You posit that _____
_____. Even so, _____
_____.

Disagree Argument 2
To add to our first point, _____
_____.

Rebuttal 3
Despite your claim that _____
_____,
we feel _____.

Disagree Argument 3
Lastly, _____
_____.

Disagree Closing Statement
To summarize, we maintain that _____
_____.

Sum Up the Debate

Finish the debate summary.

AGREEING SIDE'S ARGUMENT

The motion for this debate was _____.
The first team's main opinion was _____.
To begin with, they claimed that _____.
For example, _____
_____
Next, they explained _____.
To be more specific, _____
_____
For their third reason, they claimed that _____.
This was explained by mentioning that _____
_____.

DISAGREEING SIDE'S ARGUMENT

In contrast, the con team posited that _____
_____.
They began by arguing that _____.
To be specific, _____
_____.
For their second argument, they presented _____.
They mentioned _____
_____ to support their claim.
Finally, they said that _____.
The example they gave was _____
_____.

Unit 06 Human Cloning

A. Discuss the following questions as a class.
1. What do you see in the picture above?
2. What kind of research do you think the scientist is working on?
3. How can studying DNA and the human body change people's lives?

B. Answer the following questions with a partner.
1. Do you think it is possible to make a clone of a human being?
2. Would you want to have a clone of yourself? Why or why not?
3. Should there be laws against making human clones?

Unit 06 A Learning about the Topic

Should scientists be allowed to clone human beings?

Read the passage and underline the main ideas.

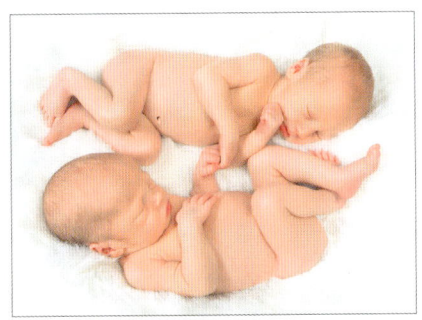

In 1997, Dolly the sheep became the first cloned mammal. The success of this experiment led scientists to wonder about the cloning of human beings. Today, people are primarily concerned about reproductive cloning. This is where an **exact** copy of a parent is created. Many argue that allowing reproductive cloning will decrease the value of human life. Still others are convinced that the possibilities of cloning make it worth exploring in spite of the potential drawbacks. To reach a conclusion, both sides of the debate must be considered.

The fact that cloning is unsafe is the primary argument against its use. The nuclear transfer technology currently used to create clones is highly **inefficient**. This can result in the creation of living organisms that are severely deformed or die. In the case of Dolly the sheep, 277 embryos were injected with the parent's DNA. Just one of these embryos survived. Such a loss of life is tragic and unnecessary. It must also be pointed out that the clones that survive may not live to be as healthy as naturally born children. Clones would be created from copied cells. These cells would have more mutations than naturally produced cells. Because of this, there is the possibility that cloned humans may age more quickly. They could also suffer from more health problems. Moreover, the value of life could become less because of human cloning. This is why the Catholic Church and UNESCO argue that cloning violates human **dignity**.

In spite of these arguments, a significant number of people support cloning. One reason is that cloning will allow scientists to **eliminate** diseases. As scientists study DNA, they will learn which genes are responsible for causing diseases. By removing these genes from people's DNA, clones would no longer have to suffer from the diseases that **plague** humanity today. We must also consider that cloning would not replace natural reproduction. Instead, it would benefit the small number of people who need cloning. This would include couples that are incapable of having children naturally. The vast majority of people would probably still prefer natural reproduction. Another argument is that clones would still be individuals. Even though cloned children would be copies of their parents, they would still have their own thoughts, ideas, and outlooks on life.

Vocabulary Check

Choose the correct word for each definition.

| exact | inefficient | dignity | eliminate | plague |

1. to cause repeated trouble or illness _____
2. to remove something that is not needed _____
3. the quality of being worthy of honor or respect _____
4. fully and completely correct _____
5. not able to work without wasting time or energy _____

Comprehension Questions

Check the correct answer for each question.

1. Why is reproductive cloning inefficient?
   - ☐ Because it requires nuclear transfer technology
   - ☐ Because most of the clones are deformed or die

2. What physical problems would clones face during their lives?
   - ☐ They would age more quickly and have more health problems.
   - ☐ They would have less dignity than naturally born children.

3. How could cloning help scientists get rid of diseases?
   - ☐ It would help them develop new medicines that make people's genes stronger.
   - ☐ It would allow them to remove the genes that cause disease from people's DNA.

4. Which of the following is true about cloned children?
   - ☐ They would become more popular than babies that are born naturally.
   - ☐ They would have different opinions about the world than their parents.

Questions for Debate

Think of and share ideas to explore the debatable issues in the article. Be sure to state your opinion clearly and to provide one supporting idea for each opinion.

1. What are some reasons you think that people would have themselves cloned?

   I think that _____

   _____.

   To be more specific, _____

   _____.

2. In your opinion, would cloned children be treated differently than naturally born children? Explain.

   It is my opinion that _____

   _____.

   The reason is _____

   _____.

3. How do you think clones would feel if they knew they were simply copies of their parents?

   My feeling about this point is _____

   _____.

   For instance, _____

   _____.

4. Some people believe people could make clones of themselves so that they could have replacement organs if they get sick. Do you feel this is a good thing to do?

   To me, it seems that _____

   _____.

   Consider that _____

   _____.

5. Should the government regulate human cloning? Why or why not?

   In this situation, it is probably best _____

   _____.

   More specifically, _____

   _____.

Opinion Examples

Look at the opinion examples about the motion below and answer the questions.

Motion: Reproductive cloning is immoral and should not be allowed.

Opinion A Track 17

A lot of the criticism about reproductive cloning is unfair. Even though it has some drawbacks, overall, reproductive cloning is beneficial. For one, think of the health benefits. Clones have the same DNA as their parents. This means that if they ever need a new organ, such as a liver or heart, they could get one quickly and easily. Cloning will also help us get rid of the genes in our DNA that cause illnesses. I also think that it should be an individual's right to have a clone made. People would have to give their own DNA and pay their own money to have clones made. No one really suffers in that situation.

Opinion B Track 18

I don't know how anyone would think that cloning is a good idea. Life is a special gift that we should all appreciate. Cloning turns the creation of life into a manufacturing process. This is why the Catholic Church and UNESCO are against human cloning. We should also oppose cloning since it results in the loss of life. Some people say embryos are not life. I disagree. The fact that up to hundreds of embryos may not survive the cloning process is frightening. Those embryos have the right to grow up and to live normal lives, just like anyone else. We must ban cloning in order to save lives.

1 Underline the main idea of each opinion.

2 Which opinion is for the topic? Which one is against it?
- FOR: _____
- AGAINST: _____

3 What supporting ideas does each opinion give?
- Opinion A: _____
- Opinion B: _____

4 Create one more supporting idea for each argument.
- Opinion A: _____
- Opinion B: _____

Skills for Debate

Read and learn how to explain a process in your reasons.

How Can You Explain a Process in Your Reasons?

Another strategy to use when explaining a process is to use **inductive reasoning**. This is when you explain a series of **facts** or **assumptions** that logically connect with each other. These ideas lead to a conclusion that connects the **subject of the first idea** to the **argument of the final idea**. For example:

   A: Socrates is a man. → B: All men are mortal. → Conc: Therefore, Socrates is mortal.

The first argument explains that Socrates is a man. The second point explains a fact about men: They are mortal. For these reason, we can conclude that Socrates is mortal.

Practicing Debate Skills

Read each of the arguments below and examine their reasons. Use inductive reasoning to connect the given first reasons to the conclusions.

1 Argument: Cloning research will allow scientists to eliminate diseases.

   Reasons: ⓐ Creating clones requires scientists to alter our DNA.

   ⓑ _____

   ⓒ _____

   ⓓ Therefore, creating clones will get rid of diseases.

2 Argument: The value of human life will decrease because of cloning.

   Reasons: ⓐ Cloning will make it possible to manufacture human beings.

   ⓑ _____

   ⓒ _____

   ⓓ Consequently, cloning will reduce the value and dignity of human life.

3 Argument: Cloned people will still have their own characteristics.

   Reasons: ⓐ Clones will grow up in different environments than their parents.

   ⓑ _____

   ⓒ _____

   ⓓ As a result, clones will have their own outlooks on life.

Unit 06 B Debating the Topic

Creating Your Debate

Motion: Reproductive cloning is immoral and should not be allowed.

What are your arguments? Get into two groups and plan for the debate. Decide whether your team is FOR (agree) or AGAINST (disagree) the motion. Then, create your ARE: Argument, Reason, and Example. Use the example arguments below and the research from your workbook to help create your arguments.

■ Example Arguments

FOR

Argument

Reproductive cloning would result in the deaths of many living beings.

Reason

The cloning process is imperfect. When scientists try to create clones, many of the clones do not develop correctly. Because of this, the clones often die. This is a tragic loss of life that is unacceptable.

Example

To create Dolly the sheep, 277 sheep embryos were used. Just one of these embryos grew into a healthy sheep. The other 276 embryos did not survive.

AGAINST

Argument

Cloning technology is improving and becoming safer.

Reason

When a technology is first used, it is experimental and imperfect. Since it is imperfect, many mistakes and problems occur. However, as scientists become better at using technology, they make fewer mistakes.

Example

More recent cloning experiments have been more efficient. In one experiment, scientists used 95 embryos to create nine milk cows. As scientists clone more, the technology will improve further.

Arguments FOR/AGAINST the Motion

ARGUMENT 1

Argument

_____
_____
_____
_____
_____
_____

Reason

_____
_____
_____
_____
_____
_____

Example

_____
_____
_____
_____
_____
_____

ARGUMENT 2

Argument

_____
_____
_____
_____
_____
_____

Reason

_____
_____
_____
_____
_____
_____

Example

_____
_____
_____
_____
_____
_____

ARGUMENT 3

Argument

_____
_____
_____
_____
_____
_____

Reason

_____
_____
_____
_____
_____
_____

Example

_____
_____
_____
_____
_____
_____

Actual Debate

Now, it's time to debate. Use the flow chart below to help you organize the debate.
The introductory expressions have been provided to help you. Put your arguments in logical order and make clear rebuttals to the opposing team's arguments.

Agree Opening Statement
From our perspective, it is clear that _____.

Agree Argument 1
Our opening argument is _____.

Rebuttal 1
Unfortunately, your argument is flawed. _____.

Agree Argument 2
The next point we would like to mention is _____.

Rebuttal 2
Even though _____, we must point out that _____.

Agree Argument 3
Finally, _____.

Agree Closing Statement
We, the members of the pro team, feel that _____.

Disagree Opening Statement
We feel that _____ should be allowed.

Rebuttal 1
The pro side's argument that _____ is flawed because _____.

Disagree Argument 1
The first reason we support this is _____.

Rebuttal 2
Our opponents are mistaken once again. The truth is _____.

Disagree Argument 2
Second of all, _____.

Rebuttal 3
The opposing team claims that _____.

Disagree Argument 3
Our concluding argument is _____.

Disagree Closing Statement
It is our overall belief that _____.

Sum Up the Debate

Finish the debate summary.

AGREEING SIDE'S ARGUMENT

The topic of today's debate was _____.

The main opinion of the agreeing team was _____.

For their first argument, they claimed _____.

This was explained by _____
_____.

Second, they argued that _____.

For example, _____
_____
_____.

Their third point was _____.

They elaborated upon this by mentioning that _____
_____.

DISAGREEING SIDE'S ARGUMENT

The con team felt differently. They argued _____
_____.

They began by stating that _____
_____.

For instance, _____
_____.

Second, they posited that _____.

They specifically mentioned _____
_____ was their final point.

In detail, they explained that _____
_____.

Chapter 4

Creating Personal Experience Examples

Unit 07 Immigration

Unit 08 Advertising Directed at Children

Unit 07 Immigration

A. Discuss the following questions as a class.
1. What do you see in the picture above?
2. Where do you think these people are originally from?
3. Why do you think the American flag is in the background?

B. Answer the following questions with a partner.
1. What are some reasons that people would choose to immigrate to another country?
2. What are some benefits that occur because of immigration?
3. What are some drawbacks that occur because of immigration?

Unit 07 A Learning about the Topic

Should nations allow immigration to continue?

Read the passage and underline the main ideas. 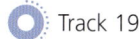 Track 19

The world today is becoming a more globalized place. Even traditionally **homogeneous** countries such as South Korea have seen a rise in immigration. The country currently has over one million foreign immigrants, and that number is likely to continue to increase. This leads to many important questions. Do nations benefit from immigration? What are some potential problems that immigration can cause? And, most significantly, should immigration between nations be allowed to continue?

Immigration allows people to improve their lives. Many immigrants are economic migrants. These are people who leave their home countries in search of higher-paying jobs and better **prospects** in other nations. This is why people emigrate from Mexico to the United States or from Vietnam to South Korea. Nations can also benefit from the work of immigrants. Less developed countries can hire workers from more developed countries who have specialized skills. This is what Singapore did. It hired foreign workers to teach them about engineering and business management. Today, Singapore is one of the world's wealthiest nations. Immigration can also lead to cultural diversity. Immigrants from other nations bring their customs, languages, foods, and cultures with them. People from nearly every nation in the world live in New York City, making the city a **melting pot** of cultures and ideas.

Nevertheless, some people are strictly opposed to immigration. In some countries, immigrants are **entitled to** more benefits than local people are. For instance, the United Kingdom used to offer free housing, medical treatment, and education to immigrant families. This caused **native** people to complain that immigrants received too many benefits. Nations can also suffer "brain drain." This occurs when well-educated people with important skills move to other nations where they can earn more money. This has happened in India, where thousands of doctors and engineers have left the country to work in wealthier nations. The result is that India lacks qualified doctors and engineers. Many also worry that too much immigration can lead to the loss of a nation's unique culture. Nations that have a strong national identity, such as in South Korea and Japan, often worry about this the most.

Vocabulary Check

Choose the correct word for each definition.

| homogenous | prospect | melting pot | entitled to | native |

1 to be allowed to have or use _____
2 an opportunity for something to happen _____
3 a place where different types of people live together _____
4 referring to the place a person was born and raised _____
5 made up of the same kind of people or things _____

Comprehension Questions

Check the correct answer for each question.

1 What are economic migrants?
　☐ People who are hired by less developed countries to teach them special skills
　☐ People who leave their native nations to find better jobs in other countries

2 Which city is considered to be a melting pot?
　☐ Singapore
　☐ New York City

3 Why did people in the United Kingdom complain about immigrants?
　☐ Because they received more benefits than native British people
　☐ Because they wanted free housing, medical treatment, and education

4 What problem does India face today?
　☐ It does not have enough qualified doctors and engineers.
　☐ It is losing its unique national identity and culture.

Questions for Debate

Think of and share ideas to explore the debatable issues in the article. Be sure to state your opinion clearly and to provide one supporting idea for each opinion.

1 Why do you think people immigrate to other countries?

My feeling is that _____
_____.

I feel this way since _____
_____.

2 Should there be laws or restrictions on immigration? Why or why not?

It seems to me that _____
_____.

For example, _____
_____.

3 How can nations benefit from hiring immigrant workers?

From my perspective, it is clear that _____
_____.

To be more specific, _____
_____.

4 Do you think it is fair for countries to give benefits such as free health care to immigrants?

My opinion is _____
_____.

One example is _____
_____.

5 Is it possible for countries to lose their national identity because of immigration? Why or why not?

There is no doubt that _____
_____.

To give you an idea, consider that _____
_____.

Opinion Examples

Look at the opinion examples about the motion below and answer the questions.

Motion: Immigration offers major benefits for both individuals and nations.

Opinion A Track 20

I understand that people want to immigrate to other nations to improve their lives, but that is not a good enough reason for it to continue. Oftentimes, native people suffer because of immigration. Immigrants come and take jobs from local people. Some immigrants will work for less money, so they decrease wages. Other times, educated immigrants take high-paying jobs, such as doctors and engineers. Either way, there are fewer jobs for native citizens. Another problem is that immigrants can get lots of benefits from the state. In some nations, immigrants are given free housing, medical care, and education. They can even get these benefits when they don't have jobs or pay taxes. This is not fair for native citizens of a nation.

Opinion B Track 21

Some of the most interesting places in the world are those that have large immigrant communities. This is why I think immigration is such a great thing. Immigration allows for a blending of cultures that would otherwise be impossible. For instance, in London, there are about 300 different languages spoken because there are so many immigrants. This means that people can enjoy food and cultural events from nations all over the world. But it also makes people more tolerant. As people become used to living with other people from different nations, they can learn to accept others' differences and to respect the our world's cultures. In a world with too much hate, immigration makes people much more tolerant and loving.

1 Underline the main idea of each opinion.

2 Which opinion is for the topic? Which one is against it?
- FOR: _____
- AGAINST: _____

3 What supporting ideas does each opinion give?
- Opinion A: _____
- Opinion B: _____

4 Create one more supporting idea for each argument.
- Opinion A: _____
- Opinion B: _____

Skills for Debate

Read and learn how to create personal experience examples.

How Can You Create Personal Experience Examples?

A simple and effective way to support your arguments is through the use of personal experience examples. Introduce your personal experience by using **transition phrases**. Some good phrases to use include, "To share my personal experience," "This was true in my case," and "I have a personal experience which relates to this point." It is also important to explain clearly the **key details** of your experience. Always explain **what** you did and **why** it is important to your argument. You can also add **when** and **where** your experience happened for more detail.

Practicing Debate Skills

Read each of the arguments below and create a personal experience example for each. Finish the transition phrase for each example and add key details. Some words have been provided to help you.

1 **Argument:** Moving to a foreign country lets people experience another culture.

   Example: • *Transition*: To give a _____
   - *what*: moved abroad to the United States _____
   - *where*: lived in the state of California in the city of _____
   - *when*: _____
   - *why*: _____

2 **Argument:** People who immigrate to another nation can have a hard time fitting in.

   Example: • *Transition*: Allow me to explain _____
   - *what*: _____
   - *where*: _____
   - *when*: moved when I was eight years old _____
   - *why*: because my father got a new job _____

3 **Argument:** People can get a better job or education by moving to a foreign nation.

   Example: • *Transition*: This was true in _____
   - *what*: _____
   - *where*: _____
   - *when*: _____
   - *why*: _____

Unit 07 B Debating the Topic

Creating Your Debate

Motion: Immigration offers major benefits for both individuals and nations.

What are your arguments? Get into two groups and plan for the debate. Decide whether your team is FOR (agree) or AGAINST (disagree) the motion. Then, create your ARE: Argument, Reason, and Example. Use the example arguments below and the research from your workbook to help create your arguments.

- **Example Arguments**

FOR

Argument

By moving to another country, people can improve their quality of life.

Reason

People generally immigrate to wealthier nations. They do this to have better lives for themselves and their families. In richer countries, people can have bigger homes, eat better food, and enjoy a wide variety of products and services.

Example

When I was younger, my family lived in Canada. There, we had a house with a huge yard. We could also eat many different foods and buy products that are not available in Korea.

AGAINST

Argument

Immigrants to a new nation can have a hard time adjusting to the country's society.

Reason

People who spend most of their lives living in one nation become used to their home country's culture. The customs and behavior of their home country are part of their character. Learning another culture is very difficult, especially when people are older.

Example

My family and I moved to Germany. We had trouble finding food we liked to eat and did not understand a lot of the customs. As a result, we mostly spent time with other Koreans.

Arguments FOR/AGAINST the Motion

ARGUMENT 1

Argument

_____
_____
_____
_____
_____

Reason

_____
_____
_____
_____
_____

Example

_____
_____
_____
_____
_____

ARGUMENT 2

Argument

_____
_____
_____
_____
_____

Reason

_____
_____
_____
_____
_____

Example

_____
_____
_____
_____
_____

ARGUMENT 3

Argument

_____
_____
_____
_____
_____

Reason

_____
_____
_____
_____
_____

Example

_____
_____
_____
_____
_____

Actual Debate

Now, it's time to debate. Use the flow chart below to help you organize the debate.
The introductory expressions have been provided to help you. Put your arguments in logical order and make clear rebuttals to the opposing team's arguments.

Agree Opening Statement
It is our central belief that _____.

Agree Argument 1
We would like to begin by mentioning that _____
_____
_____
_____.

Rebuttal 1
Your opinion that _____
_____ is mistaken.
_____.

Agree Argument 2
The next point we would like to mention is ___
_____.

Rebuttal 2
Once again, we have to disagree. We think that _____
_____.

Agree Argument 3
Our third argument is _____
_____
_____.

Agree Closing Statement
Despite our opponent's arguments, we still believe that _____
_____.

Disagree Opening Statement
We feel the exact opposite. Our main opinion is that _____
_____.

Rebuttal 1
Your argument that _____
_____
is flawed because _____.

Disagree Argument 1
Our starting argument is _____
_____.

Rebuttal 2
You contend that _____
_____, yet
_____.

Disagree Argument 2
Second of all, _____
_____.

Rebuttal 3
To us, it seems that _____
_____ is not the case since
_____.

Disagree Argument 3
To give our final point, consider that _____
_____.

Disagree Closing Statement
To summarize, we hold that _____
_____.

Sum Up the Debate

Finish the debate summary.

AGREEING SIDE'S ARGUMENT

The motion for this debate was _____.

The pro team's members argued _____.

The first point they made was _____.

For example, _____

_____.

Next, they explained _____.

To go into more detail, _____

_____.

For their final point, they stated _____.

More specifically, they claimed that _____

_____.

DISAGREEING SIDE'S ARGUMENT

In contrast, the con team posited that _____

_____.

The first argument they made was _____.

They mentioned _____

_____ to strengthen their point.

For their second argument, they presented _____.

To share their example, they said _____

_____.

They concluded by arguing that _____.

For instance, _____

_____.

Unit 08
Advertising Directed at Children

A. Discuss the following questions as a class.
1. What do you see in the picture above?
2. Why do you think the girl wants this product?
3. Do you think that advertisements make children want products they do not need?

B. Answer the following questions with a partner.
1. What are some children's products that you have seen advertised on television?
2. Why do you think that companies create advertisements for children?
3. Is it okay to create advertisements that target children? Why or why not?

Unit 08 A Learning about the Topic

Should companies be allowed to create children's advertisements?

Read the passage and underline the main ideas.

 Track 22

What do Mickey Mouse, Ronald McDonald, and the Energizer Bunny all have in common? They are characters that companies use to make their products **appealing** to children. A number of people oppose advertising to young children. They say these companies are taking advantage of children's immaturity. Defenders claim that they are simply doing what is necessary to remain competitive in today's commercial society. Which side is right? Read on to find out.

Opponents of children's advertising believe that they **exploit** children. Young children are **innocent**, so they do not understand what advertising is. This makes them more likely to be influenced by commercials. One consequence of this is that children can develop poor lifestyle habits. It is also unethical for companies to advertise to children as they have no money of their own to purchase items. After seeing ads on television, children have to ask their parents to buy the products. This could lead to unhealthy relationship between parents and their children. Some countries have already taken steps to ban advertising directed at children. Sweden restricts companies from showing advertisements during children's programming. After the ban, Swedish children under the age of 12 wanted fewer toys than children in Britain, where children's advertising is allowed.

Of course, children's advertising serves some key purposes. Advertising is already a major part of the lives of children. By one estimate, children are exposed to up to 3,000 advertisements a day. Should advertisements be banned, children would be **shielded** from reality. This could harm their development. The reason is they would not understand how our commercial society works. Even more critically, banning companies from advertising to children would be restricting freedom of speech. Most societies permit speech as long as it is not directly harmful. Children's advertising is not harmful in itself. Therefore, banning it is wrong. It must also be noted that television stations rely on advertising to generate **revenues** to support their programming. Without children's ads, stations would show fewer programs or reduce the quality of their programming. This is clearly not in the public interest.

Vocabulary Check

Choose the correct word for each definition.

| appealing | exploit | innocent | shielded | revenue |

1 to use something in a way that helps you unfairly _____

2 having qualities that people like; attractive _____

3 money that is made by a business or organization _____

4 lacking experience with the bad things of the world _____

5 protected or covered from harm _____

Comprehension Questions

Check the correct answer for each question.

1 Why are children more likely to be influenced by commercials?
   - ☐ Because their parents can easily buy the products they see in advertisements
   - ☐ Because they may not understand what advertising is

2 What happened after Sweden banned children's advertising?
   - ☐ Television channels began showing fewer children's programs.
   - ☐ Children younger than 12 years old wanted fewer toys.

3 How could banning children's advertising harm the development of children?
   - ☐ They would have a difficult time understanding how advertising is used in society.
   - ☐ They would not be allowed to express their ideas freely even if they do not harm anyone.

4 What could be an unwanted side effect of banning children's advertising?
   - ☐ Children would be exposed to fewer than 3,000 advertisements a day.
   - ☐ Television stations would show fewer or lower quality children's shows.

Questions for Debate

Think of and share ideas to explore the debatable issues in the article. Be sure to state your opinion clearly and to provide one supporting idea for each opinion.

1. What are some children's products that you have seen advertisements for? What did the ads look like?

   Some of the products I have seen advertised are _____.

   One of the ads had _____.

2. Do you think children need to be protected from the culture of advertising and spending money?

   From my perspective, it seems that _____.

   To give an example, _____.

3. Is it okay for governments to restrict children's advertising?

   I think that _____.

   I feel this way because _____.

4. Do you feel that advertisements make you want to have certain products? Why or why not?

   My experience is _____.

   For instance, _____.

5. In your opinion, is it necessary to completely ban children's advertising, or are restrictions enough?

   My feeling is _____.

   To be more specific, _____.

Opinion Examples

Look at the opinion examples about the motion below and answer the questions.

> **Motion: Children's advertisements are harmful to children and should be banned.**

Opinion A Track 23

People like to criticize children's advertising. The fact is that advertising is an important part of our society. It's best that children learn about advertising from an early age. This will help them develop good habits regarding advertising. They will learn not to be too easily influenced by ads. And just because children see ads on television doesn't mean that their parents will buy every toy they ask for. This teaches children another important lesson, which is self-discipline. To share my experience, I used to ask my parents for all the toys I saw on TV. Needless to say, they didn't buy all of them for me. Eventually, I learned to ask for a more appropriate amount of toys.

Opinion B Track 24

Children's advertising is wrong and should be outlawed. Young children are too innocent to understand what advertising is when they see it. They think that advertisements are parts of the television shows they watch. Even though they don't understand ads, they are still influenced by them. For instance, I always wanted to eat McDonald's when I was young because of ads featuring Ronald McDonald. This brings me to my next point. Children's advertising can harm the relationship between parents and children. Children will see ads and want to have lots of toys and products. So they will bother their parents until they buy them what they want.

1 Underline the main idea of each opinion.

2 Which opinion is for the topic? Which one is against it?
- FOR: _____
- AGAINST: _____

3 What supporting ideas does each opinion give?
- Opinion A: _____
- Opinion B: _____

4 Create one more supporting idea for each argument.
- Opinion A: _____
- Opinion B: _____

Skills for Debate

Read and learn how to create personal experience examples.

How Can You Create Personal Experience Examples?

An important point to remember when you use personal experience examples is that you must explain their **relevance**. After describing a **specific situation** that you experienced, you must clearly show how this relates to your argument. To do this, you must **draw parallels** between your experience and your argument. You can do this by using comparison phrases including "like" and "such as." You can also simply describe your experience in a way that is logically relevant. After making your comparisons, **reach a conclusion** that restates your main argument.

Practicing Debate Skills

Read the arguments below. Create personal experience examples for each one. List the situations, draw parallels, and reach conclusions. An example and some phrases are given to help you.

1. Advertising to children causes them to develop bad habits and desires.
   - situation: When I saw children's ads for unhealthy junk foods and toys, I wanted to have them.
   - parallel: Just like me, children who see children's advertisements will want these harmful products.
   - conclusion: Consequently, we can see that children's advertising creates harmful desires in children.

2. Children are able to tell the difference between television programs and ads from a young age.
   - situation: To share my situation,
   - parallel: Likewise, it is true that
   - conclusion: My situation shows that

3. Children's advertising can lead to bad relationships between children and their parents.
   - situation: In my case,
   - parallel: This can lead to problems such as
   - conclusion: From my experience, we can see that

Unit 08 B Debating the Topic

Creating Your Debate

Motion: Children's advertisements are harmful to children and should be banned.

What are your arguments? Get into two groups and plan for the debate. Decide whether your team is FOR (agree) or AGAINST (disagree) the motion. Then, create your ARE: Argument, Reason, and Example. Use the example arguments below and the research from your workbook to help create your arguments.

■ **Example Arguments**

FOR

Argument

Children's advertisements can harm parent-child relationships.

Reason

Advertisements make children want more toys, games, and junk food. Children will then ask their parents to buy them all of these advertised products. When children constantly ask for these products, parents can become annoyed.

Example

Starting from when I was about seven years old, I used to ask my mother to buy all the toys I saw on TV ads. At first, my mother would kindly tell me no, but then I kept asking her for more toys. After a while, she got frustrated with me.

AGAINST

Argument

Advertisements teach children about how the consumer world works.

Reason

Our world today is based on buying and consuming products. Advertisements work to introduce these products to consumers. They teach consumers about the options they have. This is an important lesson for children to learn.

Example

I see ads for all kinds of products, including toys, games, foods, and technology products. When I see these different ads, I can know which products I need and which ones I do not need.

Arguments FOR/AGAINST the Motion

ARGUMENT 1

Argument

Reason

Example

ARGUMENT 2

Argument

Reason

Example

ARGUMENT 3

Argument

Reason

Example

Actual Debate

Now, it's time to debate. Use the flow chart below to help you organize the debate.
The introductory expressions have been provided to help you. Put your arguments in logical order and make clear rebuttals to the opposing team's arguments.

Agree Opening Statement
As far as our team is concerned, _____
_____ should be banned.

Agree Argument 1
First of all, _____
_____
_____
_____
_____.

Rebuttal 1
Despite your claim that _____
_____, we feel that _____
_____.

Agree Argument 2
Another reason we favor this point is _____
_____
_____.

Rebuttal 2
You said that _____
_____.
However, we believe that _____
_____.

Agree Argument 3
The final claim we must mention is _____
_____.

Agree Closing Statement
In the end, we contend that _____
_____.

Disagree Opening Statement
Our team feels the problems of _____
_____ outweigh the benefits.

Rebuttal 1
It is wrong for you to claim that _____
_____ because _____
_____.

Disagree Argument 1
One disadvantage of _____ is
_____.

Rebuttal 2
You incorrectly assume that _____
_____. In fact, _____
_____.

Disagree Argument 2
Our second point is _____
_____.

Rebuttal 3
Despite your claim that _____
_____,
it is definitely true that _____
_____.

Disagree Argument 3
Last, but not least, _____
_____.

Disagree Closing Statement
Our overall opinion is that _____
_____.

Sum Up the Debate

Finish the debate summary.

AGREEING SIDE'S ARGUMENT

This debate topic focused on _____.

The agree team's main argument was _____.

First of all, they claimed that _____.

They mentioned _____

_____ to support this.

Next, they argued that _____.

For instance, _____

_____.

Their final point was _____.

Their supporting detail was _____

_____.

DISAGREEING SIDE'S ARGUMENT

The con team presented a completely different opinion. They argued _____

_____.

They started by positing that _____.

The detail given for this argument was _____

_____.

The second point they made was _____.

For instance, _____

_____.

Third, they said that _____

_____

_____ was mentioned to prove this point.

97

Chapter 5

Creating Factual Examples

Unit 09 Free College Education

Unit 10 Mandatory Military Service

Unit 09 — Free College Education

WARM-UP

A. Discuss the following questions as a class.
1. What do you see in the picture above?
2. Why do you think money is included in the picture?
3. What are some reasons that people go to college?

B. Answer the following questions with a partner.
1. Do you know any people who have graduated from university? If so, how did they pay for it?
2. How much do you think one year of college costs?
3. What are some ways that universities use the money they get from tuition fees?

Unit 09 A Learning about the Topic

Should college education be made free for everybody?

Read the passage and underline the main ideas.  Track 25

The average yearly university **tuition** in Denmark and Norway is just around $500. Such low tuition fees make it possible for nearly all qualified students to attend college. Compare this to the United States, where tuition costs are nearly $14,000 a year. The high tuition fees mean that U.S. colleges are some of the best in the world, but they are also too expensive for many families to afford. The solution for making college more accessible may be getting rid of tuition fees altogether.

In the United States, Japan, Mexico, and many other nations, college is very expensive. Only upper class families have enough money to pay for college outright. The rest of students need to compete for **scholarships**. If they do not get any scholarships, they must take out student loans for thousands of dollars. These loans are huge burdens and require years or even decades to pay off. By making college free, all qualified students can attend college regardless of their family background. This ensures that all citizens have a chance to succeed. Moreover, free college education benefits nations. Having more college graduates means having a larger educated workforce. These high-skilled workers can do valuable work. This work would bring in a lot of money for a nation, which justifies the high expense of free college for the state.

Critics claim that free higher education is not **viable**. The government would have to cover most of the costs if college became free. National governments would have to spend billions of dollars a year to fund free university education. Another worry is that the quality of education can suffer. To make college free, schools would have to hire fewer professors and make class sizes larger. However, many studies have shown that students learn better in smaller classes. Free higher education may have an additional **unintended** consequence: having too many educated people. If college were free, too many people would attend college. These graduates are unlikely to be willing to do jobs not requiring a degree. In some countries, this has lead to a **shortage** of manual laborers and other workers.

Vocabulary Check

Choose the correct word for each definition.

tuition	scholarship	viable	unintended	shortage

1 money given to a student to help pay for school _____
2 money paid to a school for the right to study there _____
3 a state when there is not enough of something _____
4 not planned as a purpose or a goal _____
5 capable of being done or used _____

Comprehension Questions

Check the correct answer for each question.

1 What is true about colleges in the United States?
- ☐ They are affordable for all qualified students.
- ☐ They are among the world's best colleges.

2 Why are student loans a burden for students?
- ☐ Because they can take years or decades to pay off
- ☐ Because they are only available for students from upper class families

3 How would free higher education benefit nations?
- ☐ It would produce a larger number of educated workers.
- ☐ It would create jobs for high-skilled workers.

4 What problem can occur if there are too many educated people?
- ☐ There will be too many students and not enough professors at universities.
- ☐ There will not be enough workers for jobs that do not need a degree.

Questions for Debate

Think of and share ideas to explore the debatable issues in the article. Be sure to state your opinion clearly and to provide one supporting idea for each opinion.

1. How can individuals benefit from receiving a college education?

   From my perspective, it seems that _____
   _____.

   The reason I feel this way is _____
   _____.

2. How can nations benefit when they have more college graduates?

   I believe that _____
   _____.

   For example, _____
   _____.

3. If college education were free, governments would have to raise taxes. Is this fair for all citizens? Why or why not?

   My opinion is _____
   _____.

   To give an example, _____
   _____.

4. Do you think everybody in a nation should get a university education? Explain.

   It is clear that _____
   _____.

   More specifically, _____
   _____.

5. What are some other solutions to help people afford college besides giving free tuition?

   Some other possible solutions are _____
   _____.

   For instance, _____
   _____.

Opinion Examples

Look at the opinion examples about the motion below and answer the questions.

Motion: University education should be free to help individuals and nations succeed.

Opinion A Track 26

Nearly every country in the world offers free primary and secondary education. Similarly, it is logical for them to offer free university education. The biggest advantage of no-cost higher education would be having more educated people in society. People with college degrees are able to do work that benefits a nation. For instance, they can build machines and program computers. These activities help a nation become wealthier. For this reason, governments wouldn't even have to raise taxes too much. People would automatically pay more in taxes when they earn higher salaries. And, of course, the individuals benefit by having better paying jobs and higher living standards.

Opinion B Track 27

I strongly believe that as many people should attend college as possible. However, this doesn't mean I support free college education. Quite simply, not charging tuition would be too much of a financial burden for nations. Governments would have to spend billions of dollars to make free education work. This means people must pay higher taxes. It's also important to mention that a free education would not be a very good one. Look at the quality of public schools. Oftentimes, they are not as good as private schools that charge tuition. A college education can only be high quality if the students pay for it.

1 Underline the main idea of each opinion.

2 Which opinion is for the topic? Which one is against it?
- FOR: _____
- AGAINST: _____

3 What supporting ideas does each opinion give?
- Opinion A: _____
- Opinion B: _____

4 Create one more supporting idea for each argument.
- Opinion A: _____
- Opinion B: _____

Skills for Debate

Read and learn how to create factual examples.

How Can You Create Factual Examples?

A factual example is one that relies on information that is true. A simple but effective type of factual example is the **common sense example**. Use an **idea** that is **commonly known** and **accepted to be true** to support your argument. Some phrases to use to introduce your common sense example include "We all know that," "Most people are aware that," and "It is common knowledge that." To strengthen your point further, you can also point out how the **opposite case** is **absurd** or **otherwise incorrect**. Phrases such as "Of course you would never," "It is ridiculous to think that," and "Imagine the opposite situation where" can be used to introduce this contrast.

Practicing Debate Skills

Read each of the arguments below. Use the key words to create common sense examples. You must decide which words should be used for your case and for the opposite case.

1. Making higher education free would allow all qualified students to get a college degree.

   Key Words: equal opportunity / unable to get an education / government would not provide services for citizens / qualify for better jobs

   Example: We all know that _____

   _____

   It is ridiculous to think that _____

   _____

2. Governments cannot afford to provide free college education.

   Key Words: government would have to have huge tax raises / government's budget is limited / not everybody would benefit / government has other expenses

   Example: It is common knowledge that _____

   _____

   Imagine the opposite situation where _____

   _____

Unit 09 B Debating the Topic

Creating Your Debate

Motion: University education should be free to help individuals and nations succeed.

What are your arguments? Get into two groups and plan for the debate. Decide whether your team is FOR (agree) or AGAINST (disagree) the motion. Then, create your ARE: Argument, Reason, and Example. Use the example arguments below and the research from your workbook to help create your arguments.

■ Example Arguments

FOR

Argument

Governments should provide services that benefit citizens and society.

Reason

Free higher education has clear benefits for everyone. People can live better lives, culture can develop, and nations can become wealthier. Providing free education is a sensible usage of government funding.

Example

The US government spends less than 10 billion dollars a year on funding higher education. In contrast, it spends over 800 billion dollars a year on the military. Clearly, the government can afford to spend more on college education.

AGAINST

Argument

The government can offer more grants and scholarships to make education more affordable.

Reason

Making all higher education free would not be practical. However, it is possible for the government to offer more financial assistance to students from low-income families.

Example

We all know that only some students need help paying for college. These are average students from less wealthy families. Other students with high grades can already get scholarships to pay for college. And students from wealthy families can afford to pay for college themselves.

Arguments FOR/AGAINST the Motion

ARGUMENT 1

Argument

Reason

Example

ARGUMENT 2

Argument

Reason

Example

ARGUMENT 3

Argument

Reason

Example

Actual Debate

Now, it's time to debate. Use the flow chart below to help you organize the debate.
The introductory expressions have been provided to help you. Put your arguments in logical order and make clear rebuttals to the opposing team's arguments.

Agree Opening Statement
Today, we will explain why _____.

Disagree Opening Statement
Unlike our opponents, we feel that _____.

Agree Argument 1
The first point we would like to make is _____.

Rebuttal 1
You claimed that _____.

The problem with this is _____.

Disagree Argument 1
Our opening argument is that _____.

Rebuttal 1
Despite your argument that _____, we believe that _____.

Rebuttal 2
It is incorrect to assume that _____.

Agree Argument 2
For our second argument, consider that _____.

Disagree Argument 2
Another point to consider is _____.

Rebuttal 2
Once again, we must disagree. The fact is _____.

Rebuttal 3
While the pro side feels _____, we contend that _____.

Agree Argument 3
Finally, we would like to point out that _____.

Disagree Argument 3
As for our last argument, _____.

Agree Closing Statement
We want to restate our central argument that _____.

Disagree Closing Statement
To recap, we feel that _____.

Sum Up the Debate

Finish the debate summary.

AGREEING SIDE'S ARGUMENT

Today's debate dealt with the topic of _____.

The opinion of the pro team was _____.

Their first argument was _____.

They supported this by explaining that _____
_____.

Second, they stated that _____.

The example they gave was _____
_____.

Their third reason was _____.

For example, _____
_____.

DISAGREEING SIDE'S ARGUMENT

Contrarily, the other team believed that _____
_____.

For starters, they said that _____.

Their supporting example was _____
_____.

In their second argument, they contended that _____.

For instance, _____
_____.

Finally, they posited that _____.

In detail, they explained that _____
_____.

Unit 10: Mandatory Military Service

WARM-UP

A. Discuss the following questions as a class.
1. What do you see in the picture above?
2. Why do you think the tombstones have American flags in front of them?
3. What are some of the dangers of serving in the military?

B. Answer the following questions with a partner.
1. Has anyone of your family members done mandatory military service? Who was it? How long did they serve?
2. Do you feel that national governments have a right to require citizens to be in the military?
3. Do you think mandatory military service makes a nation's military stronger or weaker?

Unit 10   A Learning about the Topic

Should countries require their citizens to serve in the military?

Read the passage and underline the main ideas.   Track 28

Mandatory military service is common throughout the world. Israel, Germany, Brazil, Russia, and South Korea are just some of the countries that have a military draft for their young people. The mandatory service periods differ but generally last from one to three years. Proponents argue that mandatory military service enhances the safety of a nation. Opponents contend that requiring military service is not necessary since voluntary militaries are sufficient. Both sides make **valid** points that must be carefully considered.

A main concern is that mandatory military service is a violation of civil liberties. In a free society, people have the right to choose what to do with their lives. The government has no place ordering citizens to fight if they do not want to. On top of this, some military experts worry that conscripted soldiers can reduce the quality of a military. Drafted soldiers are just given basic training. Often, they are not prepared for real-life combat situations. Critics argue that it would be better to **devote** more time, money, and effort to train professional soldiers. There is also the point that requiring military service can actually weaken national unity. Some people would be in favor of mandatory military service. However, a number of people would **resent** the government for making them participate in the military.

Nevertheless, requiring military service is strongly supported by many. The most obvious benefit is that it increases the size and strength of a nation's military. This is especially true with South Korea, which is still technically at war with its neighbor North Korea. The nation relies on its military draft to make sure it has a large enough fighting force to face the **threat** from the North. Mandatory military service also builds character. It teaches young people discipline. Furthermore, they learn practical skills like following orders, working as a team, and keeping a schedule. These will help them get jobs after their service time ends. Another factor to consider is **patriotism**. When military service is required, young people learn to love and respect their countries. This enhances national pride.

Vocabulary Check

Choose the correct word for each definition.

| valid | devote | resent | threat | patriotism |

1 to use time, energy, money, etc. for something _____

2 to be angry about something you think is not fair _____

3 the love that people feel for their country _____

4 the chance that something bad could happen _____

5 fair or reasonable _____

Comprehension Questions

Check the correct answer for each question.

1 Which countries require mandatory military service? Choose TWO correct answers.
 - ☐ Japan
 - ☐ Brazil
 - ☐ France
 - ☐ Russia

2 How could conscripted soldiers make the quality of a military worse?
 - ☐ They do not have enough training for actual battle situations.
 - ☐ They cost more money to train than professional soldiers.

3 Why does South Korea require military service?
 - ☐ Because there are not enough voluntary soldiers in the military
 - ☐ Because the country is still at war with North Korea

4 What practical skills do young people learn from their military service?
 - ☐ They learn to follow orders and to keep a schedule.
 - ☐ They learn to use weapons and to control military equipment.

Questions for Debate

Think of and share ideas to explore the debatable issues in the article. Be sure to state your opinion clearly and to provide one supporting idea for each opinion.

1. If you had the choice, would you want to serve in the military? Why or why not?

   In my opinion, _____.

   The reason I say this is _____.

2. Do you feel the government has a right to force its citizens to participate in the military? Explain.

   I feel that _____.

   For instance, _____.

3. What are some benefits mandatory military service has for national governments?

   From my perspective, it seems that _____.

   To go into detail, _____.

4. Do you think militaries today need a large number of soldiers since advanced weapons such as missiles are used in modern wars? Explain.

   It is my belief that _____.

   One example is _____.

5. Besides mandatory military service, what are some other duties national governments could require of their young people?

   My opinion is _____.

   The reason I believe this is _____.

Opinion Examples

Look at the opinion examples about the motion below and answer the questions.

> **Motion: Mandatory military service is no longer needed in today's society.**

Opinion A Track 29

Back when wars were still fought mostly with soldiers, having mandatory military service was a good idea. But as we all know, this is not how wars today are fought. Likewise, military conscription is no longer needed in today's society. As far as national security is concerned, it would be much better for nations to invest more in military technology such as jet fighters. This would improve national security much more. Young people themselves don't benefit much from military service either. The government should give them more scholarships and job opportunities. This will help them more in the long run than serving a couple years in the military.

Opinion B Track 30

Even though mandatory military service doesn't really help nations win wars anymore, it is still a good idea and should continue. First of all, mandatory service makes citizens appreciate their lives and freedom more. They learn the cost and effort required to keep their nation safe. What's more, young people can learn important life skills that help them become mature. They learn discipline. They learn how to follow orders. They learn to keep a strict schedule. These are all important skills that some people may never learn without military service. Overall, mandatory military service makes the people of a nation more loyal and dedicated citizens.

1 Underline the main idea of each opinion.

2 Which opinion is for the topic? Which one is against it?
- FOR: _____
- AGAINST: _____

3 What supporting ideas does each opinion give?
- Opinion A: _____
- Opinion B: _____

4 Create one more supporting idea for each argument.
- Opinion A: _____
- Opinion B: _____

Skills for Debate

Read and learn how to create factual examples.

How Can You Create Factual Examples?

Factual examples can also be about **specific information**. In your example, you should mention true events that relate to your argument and prove why it is correct. The information can be widely known, but you must be sure to choose only the **relevant details** about your fact to support your idea. Do not include all details; only include those that prove your argument. When creating factual examples, it is important to do **research**. Some of the sources you should use include **newspapers, online news sites, encyclopedias,** and **books**.

Practicing Debate Skills

Read the news article below. Choose the relevant details and create examples for the two given arguments.

> The American people began to oppose mandatory military service in the late 1960s because of the Vietnam War. In 1973, President Richard Nixon finally cancelled the military draft. Decades later, mandatory military service is still unpopular. The fact is that many young people view mandatory military service as wasted time. This is not surprising. Conscripted soldiers have to sleep with strangers, wake up early, and run long distances while carrying heavy equipment. They are often assigned to faraway military bases where they have few chances to see their family. Their work includes jobs such as guard duty, preparing food, and cleaning bathrooms. These are simple tasks that do not teach many valuable skills to young people. Today, many people believe that the government does not have the right to tell them how to live their lives. For this reason, the draft is unlikely to come back any time soon.

1. **Argument:** Mandatory military service is too stressful and difficult for most young people.

    Example: To share a specific fact, it is true that _____

    _____

    _____

2. **Argument:** Requiring military service is not popular with most people.

    Example: One situation that illustrates my argument is _____

    _____

    _____

Unit 10 B Debating the Topic

Creating Your Debate

Motion: Mandatory military service is no longer needed in today's society.

What are your arguments? Get into two groups and plan for the debate. Decide whether your team is FOR (agree) or AGAINST (disagree) the motion. Then, create your ARE: Argument, Reason, and Example. Use the example arguments below and the research from your workbook to help create your arguments.

■ Example Arguments

FOR

Argument

People in a free society should be allowed to choose how to live their lives.

Reason

Most nations in today's world allow people to live their lives as they want. The government does not have the right to make people do something they do not want to do. This is definitely the case with military service since many people are opposed to violence and war.

Example

President Richard Nixon cancelled the draft in 1973 because it was so unpopular. Millions of Americans considered requiring military service as going against the idea of personal freedom.

AGAINST

Argument

Citizens must be willing to defend their nation in order to enjoy the benefits of living there.

Reason

Governments provide a lot of rights to their people. Therefore, it is logical for them to have certain expectations for their citizens. This includes the expectation of military service.

Example

As the old saying goes, "Freedom isn't free." Like it or not, world peace is the result of war. The young people of a nation must be willing to fight in order to keep their freedom.

Arguments FOR/AGAINST the Motion

ARGUMENT 1

Argument

Reason

Example

ARGUMENT 2

Argument

Reason

Example

ARGUMENT 3

Argument

Reason

Example

Actual Debate

Now, it's time to debate. Use the flow chart below to help you organize the debate.
The introductory expressions have been provided to help you. Put your arguments in logical order and make clear rebuttals to the opposing team's arguments.

Agree Opening Statement
Regarding the issue of _____,
it is our team's belief that _____
_____.

Disagree Opening Statement
We feel the opposite. To us, it is clear that _____
_____.

Agree Argument 1
Our opening argument is _____
_____
_____
_____
_____.

Rebuttal 1
Your statement that _____
_____ is incorrect because
_____.

Disagree Argument 1
To share our first point, _____
_____.

Rebuttal 1
Your opinion that _____
_____ is mistaken.
_____.

Rebuttal 2
You argue that _____
_____.
Yet _____.

Agree Argument 2
The next point we want to make is _____
_____.

Disagree Argument 2
Second of all, _____
_____.

Rebuttal 2
The idea that _____
_____ is wrong because
_____.

Rebuttal 3
Despite your argument that _____
_____, we believe _____
_____.

Agree Argument 3
For our last argument, let us point out that _____
_____.

Disagree Argument 3
Our third and final argument is _____
_____.

Agree Closing Statement
Our overall opinion remains that _____
_____.

Disagree Closing Statement
In conclusion, it is clear that _____
_____.

Sum Up the Debate

Finish the debate summary.

AGREEING SIDE'S ARGUMENT

The motion for this debate was _____.

The pro team argued that _____.

Their first argument was _____.

For example, _____
_____.

Next, they explained _____.

More specifically, _____
_____.

The third reason they mentioned was _____.

In detail, _____
_____.

DISAGREEING SIDE'S ARGUMENT

The second team felt differently. They stated that _____
_____.

The opening argument they gave was _____.

They mentioned _____
_____ to support their claim.

Second, they stated that _____.

Their example was _____
_____.

For their final argument, they mentioned that _____.

For instance, _____
_____.

Instilling Knowledge and Skills
for Thoughtful Debate

DEBATE Pro

Book 3

Jonathan S. McClelland

Workbook

DARAKWON

DEBATE Pro
Book 3

Workbook

DARAKWON

Contents

How to Use This Book _4

Unit 01 Public Smoking Ban _6

Unit 02 Cell Phones for Children _10

Unit 03 Hosting the Olympics _14

Unit 04 Alternative Energy _18

Unit 05 Standardized Tests _22

Unit 06 Human Cloning _26

Unit 07 Immigration _30

Unit 08 Advertising Directed at Children _34

Unit 09 Free College Education _38

Unit 10 Mandatory Military Service _42

How to Use This Book

Overview

The workbook is intended to supplement the main book both during class and for homework. It provides space for students to take notes during class and to do additional research outside of class.

Introduction for each section

Organizing Ideas

This part requires students to analyze the reading passage from the main book and write down each of the arguments and examples for and against the topic.

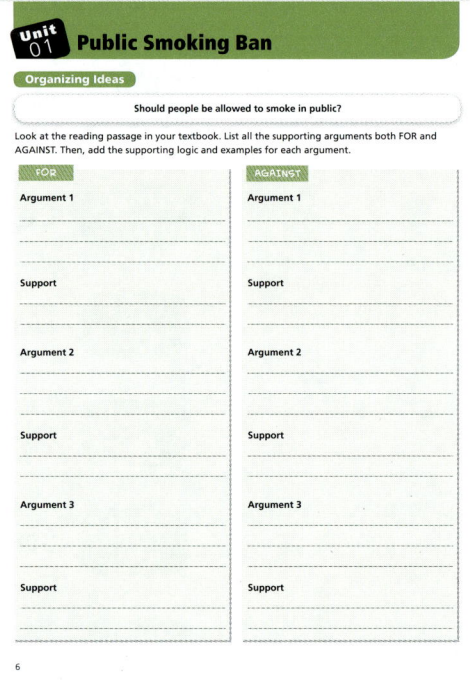

Making Supporting Examples

This section helps students develop their skills in making examples. In each book, five types of examples are explained: statistics, expert opinions, facts, academic studies, and personal opinions.

Additional Research

This section provides students with additional information about the topic based on the type of example explained in the previous section. The information is followed by four brief comprehension questions. Sample phrases are provided to help students create their answers.

Your Research

In this section, students are asked to do additional research outside of class. They are encouraged to find information from magazines, newspapers, or academic websites and to write or tape the material in the space provided. Based on the information they find, students are asked to create four additional examples which they can use during their debate.

Debate Note-Taking

This section provides space which students can use to take notes during the debate.

Peer Evaluation

This part requires students to evaluate their peers' debate performance. Eight criteria are provided along with a ten-point scale for each criterion with a total maximum score of eighty points for each student.

Unit 01 Public Smoking Ban

Organizing Ideas

Should people be allowed to smoke in public?

Look at the reading passage in your textbook. List all the supporting arguments both FOR and AGAINST. Then, add the supporting logic and examples for each argument.

FOR	AGAINST
Argument 1	**Argument 1**
Support	**Support**
Argument 2	**Argument 2**
Support	**Support**
Argument 3	**Argument 3**
Support	**Support**

Making Supporting Examples: Academic Studies

Academic studies are research that is done by universities, governments, and large research organizations. During these studies, researchers examine events to understand what causes them and why they are important. Using academic studies is a good way to strengthen your argument. Below are some academic studies related to the topic of public smoking bans.

Additional Research

Before starting your argument, let's do some extra research on the topic. Read the academic study about public smoking bans.

> One of the greatest threats to public health is exposure to secondhand smoke (SHS). In the United States alone, SHS causes around 50,000 deaths per year from cancer or heart disease. It is also responsible for between 30 to 60 percent of coronary heart disease (CHD) cases among nonsmokers. Our studies indicate that the rate of heart disease among both smokers and nonsmokers drastically decreases when the number of smoking bans increases.
>
> **Smoking Bans Becoming More Common**
> According to recent counts, 575 cities and counties in the United States have adopted a complete ban on smoking in businesses. These include workplaces, restaurants, cafés, and other indoor establishments. As the number of places with smoking bans has increased, the number of smokers has decreased. Current estimates show that fewer than 20 percent of American adults smoke. This is down from nearly 25 percent in 1997 and almost 50 percent in 1960.
>
> **Hospital Visits Down**
> The decrease in the number of smokers has had a positive influence of the health of the general population. Nationwide, admission rates for CHD-related diseases due to cigarettes have dropped greatly. From 2000 to 2010, the average rate of hospital visits dropped from 35 per 10,000 people to 21. This is nearly a 40 percent decrease. This strongly suggests that smoking bans have a positive effect on the health of the population.

Work with a partner and answer the following questions. Phrases have been provided to help you.

1 What are the leading causes of death caused by secondhand smoking?
→ *The two leading causes of death are* _____.

2 What businesses are affected by smoking bans in the United States?
→ *The smoking bans affect* _____.

3 How have smoking bans affected the number of American smokers?
→ *The number of smokers has* _____.

4 By what amount have hospital admission rates changed due to smoking bans?
→ *Hospital admission rates have* _____.

Your Research

Find an article about public smoking bans from a magazine, newspaper, or academic website. Paste or tape the article in your workbook in the space below.

Paste or Tape Your Research Article Here

Read your article and write four specific examples or pieces of evidence you can use for your debate. Try to include different types of examples, including opinion polls, statistics, academic studies, and general facts.

- _____
- _____
- _____
- _____

Debate Note-Taking

Use this page to take notes about the opposing team's arguments during the debate.

Note-Taking

Peer Evaluation

Read the assessment criteria and objectively evaluate your peers on a scale from 1 to 10.

CRITERIA	Name				
Understands the subject well	/10	/10	/10	/10	/10
Supports opinion with clear logic and examples	/10	/10	/10	/10	/10
Introduces opinions with appropriate connectors (In my view, I agree, For example, etc.)	/10	/10	/10	/10	/10
Uses a variety of vocabulary and expressions	/10	/10	/10	/10	/10
Accurately uses a variety of grammatical structures	/10	/10	/10	/10	/10
Does not monopolize the conversation and lets other people express themselves	/10	/10	/10	/10	/10
Listens attentively and respects other people's opinions	/10	/10	/10	/10	/10
Is able to accept criticism without becoming upset	/10	/10	/10	/10	/10
TOTAL SCORE	/80	/80	/80	/80	/80

Unit 02: Cell Phones for Children

Organizing Ideas

Should children be allowed to have their own cell phones?

Look at the reading passage in your textbook. List all the supporting arguments both FOR and AGAINST. Then, add the supporting logic and examples for each argument.

FOR	AGAINST
Argument 1	**Argument 1**
Support	**Support**
Argument 2	**Argument 2**
Support	**Support**
Argument 3	**Argument 3**
Support	**Support**

Making Supporting Examples: Personal Experience

Personal experience is your experience related to the topic. Using personal experience can be a good way to support your argument if you explain how your experience proves your point. However, you should be careful because one person's experience might not be common. This can actually weaken your argument. Below are some personal experiences related to the topic of cell phones for children.

Additional Research

Before starting your argument, let's do some extra research on the topic. Read the personal experiences about cell phones for children.

Somin Jung, sixth-grade student

My parents got me my first cell phone for my tenth birthday. Most of the time, I just keep my phone in my backpack. I usually use my phone to call my mother or father. Sure, I sometimes send messages to my friends and play games when I'm on the bus. But these are just ways for me to socialize and to have fun and are things that I'd do even if I didn't have a cell phone. Still, to make sure I don't use my phone too much, my parents and I came up with some rules for it. I can't play games for more than 30 minutes a day, and I can't use my phone during my study time. But I think these are good rules for me to follow and to help me be more responsible.

Justin Lee, seventh-grade student

My parents still haven't gotten me a cell phone. They say I'm too young to have one. I think they're right. A lot of my friends at school are glued to their cell phones. As soon as the bell rings and break time starts, most of my friends get on their cell phones to play games or to send messages. They don't even bother to talk with the people sitting right next to them! One boy in another class got in big trouble when he was caught using his cell phone to cheat. He was using the Internet to look up answers during a test. Cell phones are great tools, but I think children shouldn't have them until they are old enough to use them responsibly.

Work with a partner and answer the following questions. Phrases have been provided to help you.

1. For what purposes does Somin like to use her cell phone?
   → She likes to use her cell phone to _____.

2. What does Somin think of the rules about her cell phone usage?
   → She thinks that _____.

3. What happens at Justin's school during breaks between classes?
   → Most of the students _____.

4. Why did one of the students in Justin's school get in trouble?
   → He was punished because _____.

Your Research

Find an article about cell phones for children from a magazine, newspaper, or academic website. Paste or tape the article in your workbook in the space below.

Paste or Tape Your Research Article Here

Read your article and write four specific examples or pieces of evidence you can use for your debate. Try to include different types of examples, including opinion polls, statistics, academic studies, and general facts.

- _____
- _____
- _____
- _____

Debate Note-Taking

Use this page to take notes about the opposing team's arguments during the debate.

Note-Taking

Peer Evaluation

Read the assessment criteria and objectively evaluate your peers on a scale from 1 to 10.

CRITERIA	Name				
Understands the subject well	/10	/10	/10	/10	/10
Supports opinion with clear logic and examples	/10	/10	/10	/10	/10
Introduces opinions with appropriate connectors (In my view, I agree, For example, etc.)	/10	/10	/10	/10	/10
Uses a variety of vocabulary and expressions	/10	/10	/10	/10	/10
Accurately uses a variety of grammatical structures	/10	/10	/10	/10	/10
Does not monopolize the conversation and lets other people express themselves	/10	/10	/10	/10	/10
Listens attentively and respects other people's opinions	/10	/10	/10	/10	/10
Is able to accept criticism without becoming upset	/10	/10	/10	/10	/10
TOTAL SCORE	/80	/80	/80	/80	/80

Unit 03 Hosting the Olympics

Organizing Ideas

Should nations compete to host the Olympics?

Look at the reading passage in your textbook. List all the supporting arguments both FOR and AGAINST. Then, add the supporting logic and examples for each argument.

FOR

Argument 1
_____
_____
_____

Support
_____
_____
_____

Argument 2
_____
_____
_____

Support
_____
_____
_____

Argument 3
_____
_____
_____

Support
_____
_____
_____

AGAINST

Argument 1
_____
_____
_____

Support
_____
_____
_____

Argument 2
_____
_____
_____

Support
_____
_____
_____

Argument 3
_____
_____
_____

Support
_____
_____
_____

Making Supporting Examples: Statistics

Statistics are facts based on numbers. They are usually created by governments, universities, news organizations, and companies. Statistics often show the number of people, companies, and nations that agree with a certain opinion or policy. To show these numbers, statistics can include percentages, populations, and points. Below are some statistics related to the topic of hosting the Olympics.

Additional Research

Before starting your argument, let's do some extra research on the topic. Read the statistics on hosting the Olympics.

Costs and Long-Term Benefits of 2012 London Olympics

Total Cost of London Olympics: Approximately $15 billion

Short-Term Economic Impact (During the Seven Weeks during the Games)
- Increase in Economic Output: $1.7 billion
- Increase in Consumer Spending*: $1.2 billion
- Increase in U.K. Residents' Incomes: $366 million
   * Includes money spent by tourists on hotels, transportation, food, and souveneirs

Long-Term Economic Impact from 2012 to 2015
- Total Economic Growth: $8.1 billion
- Increase in Economic Growth per Year: $2.2 billion
- Additional Income for U.K. Residents per Year: $475 million
- Percent of Overall Growth for the Economy: 3.5%
- Additional Jobs per Year: 17,900

Work with a partner and answer the following questions. Phrases have been provided to help you.

1 Why will consumer spending increase so much during the Olympics?

   → It will increase so much because tourists will _____.

2 By how much will the overall economy grow in the United Kingdom from 2012 to 2015?

   → The economy will grow by _____.

3 In what ways will British residents benefit from hosting the Olympic Games?

   → The British people will _____.

4 What is the overall message of these statistics?

   → The overall message of these statistics is that _____.

Your Research

Find an article about hosting the Olympics from a magazine, newspaper, or academic website. Paste or tape the article in your workbook in the space below.

Paste or Tape Your Research Article Here

Read your article and write four specific examples or pieces of evidence you can use for your debate. Try to include different types of examples, including opinion polls, statistics, academic studies, and general facts.

- _____
- _____
- _____
- _____

Debate Note-Taking

Use this page to take notes about the opposing team's arguments during the debate.

Note-Taking

Peer Evaluation

Read the assessment criteria and objectively evaluate your peers on a scale from 1 to 10.

CRITERIA	Name				
Understands the subject well	/10	/10	/10	/10	/10
Supports opinion with clear logic and examples	/10	/10	/10	/10	/10
Introduces opinions with appropriate connectors (In my view, I agree, For example, etc.)	/10	/10	/10	/10	/10
Uses a variety of vocabulary and expressions	/10	/10	/10	/10	/10
Accurately uses a variety of grammatical structures	/10	/10	/10	/10	/10
Does not monopolize the conversation and lets other people express themselves	/10	/10	/10	/10	/10
Listens attentively and respects other people's opinions	/10	/10	/10	/10	/10
Is able to accept criticism without becoming upset	/10	/10	/10	/10	/10
TOTAL SCORE	/80	/80	/80	/80	/80

Unit 04 Alternative Energy

Organizing Ideas

Should alternative energy sources replace traditional ones?

Look at the reading passage in your textbook. List all the supporting arguments both FOR and AGAINST. Then, add the supporting logic and examples for each argument.

FOR	AGAINST
Argument 1	**Argument 1**
Support	**Support**
Argument 2	**Argument 2**
Support	**Support**
Argument 3	**Argument 3**
Support	**Support**

Making Supporting Examples: Facts

A fact is something true. For debates, you can use facts that are common knowledge, but you should also try to use more specific, less commonly known facts. The best places to find specific facts are newspaper and magazine articles. In these sources, you can find all of the details of a situation and can read interviews from people related to the story. Below are some facts related to the topic of alternative energy.

Additional Research

Before starting your argument, let's do some extra research on the topic. Read the facts about alternative energy.

Seven Facts You Should Know about Your Energy Sources

- Until the 1850s, wood supplied around 90 percent of the world's energy.
- Today, coal and oil account have replaced wood as the main source of energy. They account for about 80 percent of the world's energy supply.
- In 2010, renewable energy sources supplied about 10 percent of the energy in the United States, but that number is expected to rise.
- Over half of renewable energy sources are used to create electricity.
- The United States government has created laws, including the Energy Policy Acts of 2002 and 2005, to encourage the use of alternative energy sources by raising the price of oil and natural gas.
- In one hour, enough sunlight reaches the Earth to supply the world's energy for a year.
- About 10,000 homes in the United States get all of their energy from solar power.

Work with a partner and answer the following questions. Phrases have been provided to help you.

1 What used to be the primary source of energy? What are the prime sources today?

→ *The main source of energy until the 1850s was* _____,

  but now the main sources are _____.

2 Alternative energy sources provide what percentage of energy in the United States?

→ *They provide* _____.

3 How does the United States government feel about alternative energy sources? How do you know?

→ *The U.S. government feels that* _____.

  The reason is _____.

4 What is suggested by the following: "In one hour, enough sunlight reaches the Earth to supply the world's energy for a year"?

→ *This fact suggests that* _____.

Your Research

Find an article about alternative energy from a magazine, newspaper, or academic website. Paste or tape the article in your workbook in the space below.

Read your article and write four specific examples or pieces of evidence you can use for your debate. Try to include different types of examples, including opinion polls, statistics, academic studies, and general facts.

- _____
- _____
- _____
- _____

Debate Note-Taking

Use this page to take notes about the opposing team's arguments during the debate.

Note-Taking

Peer Evaluation

Read the assessment criteria and objectively evaluate your peers on a scale from 1 to 10.

CRITERIA	Name				
Understands the subject well	/10	/10	/10	/10	/10
Supports opinion with clear logic and examples	/10	/10	/10	/10	/10
Introduces opinions with appropriate connectors (In my view, I agree, For example, etc.)	/10	/10	/10	/10	/10
Uses a variety of vocabulary and expressions	/10	/10	/10	/10	/10
Accurately uses a variety of grammatical structures	/10	/10	/10	/10	/10
Does not monopolize the conversation and lets other people express themselves	/10	/10	/10	/10	/10
Listens attentively and respects other people's opinions	/10	/10	/10	/10	/10
Is able to accept criticism without becoming upset	/10	/10	/10	/10	/10
TOTAL SCORE	/80	/80	/80	/80	/80

Unit 05 Standardized Tests

Organizing Ideas

Should schools rely on standardized tests to evaluate students?

Look at the reading passage in your textbook. List all the supporting arguments both FOR and AGAINST. Then, add the supporting logic and examples for each argument.

FOR

Argument 1
_____
_____
_____

Support
_____
_____
_____

Argument 2
_____
_____
_____

Support
_____
_____
_____

Argument 3
_____
_____
_____

Support
_____
_____
_____

AGAINST

Argument 1
_____
_____
_____

Support
_____
_____
_____

Argument 2
_____
_____
_____

Support
_____
_____
_____

Argument 3
_____
_____
_____

Support
_____
_____
_____

Making Supporting Examples: Expert Opinions

Expert opinions are usually the ideas and opinions of experts in any given field. Experts are typically people such as professors, doctors, and business managers. Most experts base their opinions on their years of experience doing research and working in their fields. Below are some expert opinions related to the topic of standardized tests.

Additional Research

Before starting your argument, let's do some extra research on the topic. Read the expert opinions about standardized tests.

Rebecca Hamilton, Eighth-Grade English Teacher

This year, my students are going to have to take a national standardized exam. The government says that the test will help make our country's students smarter and make sure that learning standards are equal. However, I'm still not sure it will work. What ends up happening is that teachers teach to the test. That is, all the work in their classes is focused on the test material. So, in my case, I would not be able to teach poetry because poetry is not covered on the test. I'm also worried that the tests will put too much pressure on the students to get good scores. Many students already worry about their grades. They don't need the extra pressure of a standardized test in their lives.

Margaret Jackson, National Director of Standardized Testing

As the National Director of Standardized Testing, I can assure you that teachers' fears about standardized tests are unjustified. Our office works directly with teachers and education departments to make sure that our tests cover the materials that students learn in class. Teachers don't need to change their teaching styles, and students don't need to cram for these exams. As long as teachers and students are doing the work they should, they will be fine. Besides, parents also want to know what their children are learning in school and how well they are doing. Really, standardized tests are the perfect tool for parents to do just that.

Work with a partner and answer the following questions. Phrases have been provided to help you.

1. What benefits will standardized testing have according to the government?
   → The government claims that _____.

2. How will Rebecca Hamilton have to change her classes because of standardized testing?
   → She will have to _____.

3. According to Margaret Jackson, why will teachers not need to change their teaching styles?
   → She says that the standardized tests will _____.

4. How will parents be able to make use of standardized tests?
   → Parents will be able to _____.

Your Research

Find an article about standardized tests from a magazine, newspaper, or academic website. Paste or tape the article in your workbook in the space below.

Paste or Tape Your Research Article Here

Read your article and write four specific examples or pieces of evidence you can use for your debate. Try to include different types of examples, including opinion polls, statistics, academic studies, and general facts.

- _____
- _____
- _____
- _____

Debate Note-Taking

Use this page to take notes about the opposing team's arguments during the debate.

Note-Taking

___

Peer Evaluation

Read the assessment criteria and objectively evaluate your peers on a scale from 1 to 10.

CRITERIA	Name				
Understands the subject well	/10	/10	/10	/10	/10
Supports opinion with clear logic and examples	/10	/10	/10	/10	/10
Introduces opinions with appropriate connectors (In my view, I agree, For example, etc.)	/10	/10	/10	/10	/10
Uses a variety of vocabulary and expressions	/10	/10	/10	/10	/10
Accurately uses a variety of grammatical structures	/10	/10	/10	/10	/10
Does not monopolize the conversation and lets other people express themselves	/10	/10	/10	/10	/10
Listens attentively and respects other people's opinions	/10	/10	/10	/10	/10
Is able to accept criticism without becoming upset	/10	/10	/10	/10	/10
TOTAL SCORE	/80	/80	/80	/80	/80

Unit 06 Human Cloning

Organizing Ideas

Should scientists be allowed to clone human beings?

Look at the reading passage in your textbook. List all the supporting arguments both FOR and AGAINST. Then, add the supporting logic and examples for each argument.

FOR	AGAINST
Argument 1	**Argument 1**
Support	**Support**
Argument 2	**Argument 2**
Support	**Support**
Argument 3	**Argument 3**
Support	**Support**

Making Supporting Examples: Academic Studies

Academic studies are research that is done by universities, governments, and large research organizations. During these studies, researchers examine events to understand what causes them and why they are important. Using academic studies is a good way to strengthen your argument. Below are some academic studies related to the topic of human cloning.

Additional Research

Before starting your argument, let's do some extra research on the topic. Read the academic studies about human cloning.

> Cloning became a major issue in 1997 when the cloned sheep Dolly was created. National lawmakers must now decide how to regulate human cloning research. At this time, there are three main courses of action, which are:
>
> **1. A Total Ban on All Cloning**
> A total ban on all cloning would put an end to all of the research associated with cloning, including important genetic research for medicine. Since many nations already allow research on cloning, this is unlikely to occur.
>
> **2. A Ban on Reproductive Cloning**
> Currently, there is some support for a ban on reproductive cloning. Many states oppose reproductive cloning on moral grounds. A number of scientists also believe that reproductive cloning is still too unreliable at this time. In other words, it would be better for scientists to spend their time researching cloning to make it more efficient.
>
> **3. A Ban on Reproductive Cloning but the Allowing of Research Cloning**
> The most possible option is a ban on reproductive cloning while still allowing research to continue. This would enable scientists to develop new medical treatments. These include cures for diseases and growing organs for transplants. This would allow scientists to use cloning to improve human quality of life.

Work with a partner and answer the following questions. Phrases have been provided to help you.

1 What are the problems that could occur with a total ban on cloning?

→ *The problems would be* _____.

2 Why is it unlikely that a total cloning ban would occur?

→ *It is unlikely because* _____.

3 For what reason do some scientists believe that reproductive cloning is inefficient?

→ *They feel this way because* _____.

4 What are the benefits to people if cloning research is allowed to continue?

→ *The benefits are* _____.

Your Research

Find an article about human cloning from a magazine, newspaper, or academic website. Paste or tape the article in your workbook in the space below.

Paste or Tape Your Research Article Here

Read your article and write four specific examples or pieces of evidence you can use for your debate. Try to include different types of examples, including opinion polls, statistics, academic studies, and general facts.

- _____
- _____
- _____
- _____

Debate Note-Taking

Use this page to take notes about the opposing team's arguments during the debate.

Note-Taking

Peer Evaluation

Read the assessment criteria and objectively evaluate your peers on a scale from 1 to 10.

CRITERIA	Name				
Understands the subject well	/10	/10	/10	/10	/10
Supports opinion with clear logic and examples	/10	/10	/10	/10	/10
Introduces opinions with appropriate connectors (In my view, I agree, For example, etc.)	/10	/10	/10	/10	/10
Uses a variety of vocabulary and expressions	/10	/10	/10	/10	/10
Accurately uses a variety of grammatical structures	/10	/10	/10	/10	/10
Does not monopolize the conversation and lets other people express themselves	/10	/10	/10	/10	/10
Listens attentively and respects other people's opinions	/10	/10	/10	/10	/10
Is able to accept criticism without becoming upset	/10	/10	/10	/10	/10
TOTAL SCORE	/80	/80	/80	/80	/80

Unit 07 Immigration

Organizing Ideas

Should nations allow immigration to continue?

Look at the reading passage in your textbook. List all the supporting arguments both FOR and AGAINST. Then, add the supporting logic and examples for each argument.

FOR	AGAINST
Argument 1	**Argument 1**
Support	**Support**
Argument 2	**Argument 2**
Support	**Support**
Argument 3	**Argument 3**
Support	**Support**

Making Supporting Examples: Expert Opinions

Expert opinions are usually the ideas and opinions of experts in any given field. Experts are typically people such as professors, doctors, and business managers. Most experts base their opinions on their years of experience doing research and working in their fields. Below are some expert opinions related to the topic of immigration.

Additional Research

Before starting your argument, let's do some extra research on the topic. Read the expert opinions about immigration.

Chen Lee, Singapore Ministry of Finance

In 1965, Singapore's average income was only $511 per year. Today, Singapore is the third-richest nation in the world with an income of over $61,000 a year. How did Singapore become so wealthy? The answer is through immigration. In the late 1960s, Prime Minister Lee Kuan Yew asked foreign business experts to come to Singapore. They helped the nation set up factories and develop businesses. Now, nearly 40 percent of Singapore's population in foreign-born, which is the highest of any nation in the world. In addition to doing business, immigrants today also do construction and maintenance work. Immigration will help Singapore remain one of the world's richest nations.

Professor Thomas Clarkson, Sociology Professor

Around 35 percent of the people living in London were born outside the U.K. While this has contributed greatly to London's status as a world city, the huge amount of immigration has also brought problems. Primarily, foreign immigrants sometimes have difficulty fitting into British society. There are cultural differences that they are not accustomed to. They range from greetings to national laws. The language barrier is also a major issue. Many immigrants are not native English speakers, so they are sometimes unable to find jobs. When this happens, they have to rely on support from the government for housing, health care, etc.

Work with a partner and answer the following questions. Phrases have been provided to help you.

1. How has the average income in Singapore changed since 1965?
   → *In 1965, the average income was* _____.
   Today, the average person makes _____.

2. For what purposes does Singapore use foreign labor?
   → *The country uses immigrant workers to* _____.

3. Why do immigrants have a hard time fitting into British society?
   → *The main reasons are* _____.

4. What happens to immigrants who cannot find jobs due to the language barrier?
   → *They have to* _____.

Your Research

Find an article about immigration from a magazine, newspaper, or academic website. Paste or tape the article in your workbook in the space below.

Paste or Tape Your Research Article Here

Read your article and write four specific examples or pieces of evidence you can use for your debate. Try to include different types of examples, including opinion polls, statistics, academic studies, and general facts.

- _____
- _____
- _____
- _____

Debate Note-Taking

Use this page to take notes about the opposing team's arguments during the debate.

Note-Taking

Peer Evaluation

Read the assessment criteria and objectively evaluate your peers on a scale from 1 to 10.

CRITERIA	Name				
Understands the subject well	/10	/10	/10	/10	/10
Supports opinion with clear logic and examples	/10	/10	/10	/10	/10
Introduces opinions with appropriate connectors (In my view, I agree, For example, etc.)	/10	/10	/10	/10	/10
Uses a variety of vocabulary and expressions	/10	/10	/10	/10	/10
Accurately uses a variety of grammatical structures	/10	/10	/10	/10	/10
Does not monopolize the conversation and lets other people express themselves	/10	/10	/10	/10	/10
Listens attentively and respects other people's opinions	/10	/10	/10	/10	/10
Is able to accept criticism without becoming upset	/10	/10	/10	/10	/10
TOTAL SCORE	/80	/80	/80	/80	/80

Unit 08: Advertising Directed at Children

Organizing Ideas

Should companies be allowed to create children's advertisements?

Look at the reading passage in your textbook. List all the supporting arguments both FOR and AGAINST. Then, add the supporting logic and examples for each argument.

FOR	AGAINST
Argument 1	**Argument 1**
Support	**Support**
Argument 2	**Argument 2**
Support	**Support**
Argument 3	**Argument 3**
Support	**Support**

Making Supporting Examples: Personal Experience

Personal experience is your experience related to the topic. Using personal experience can be a good way to support your argument if you explain how your experience proves your point. However, you should be careful because one person's experience might not be common. This can actually weaken your argument. Below are some personal experiences related to the topic of advertising directed at children.

Additional Research

Before starting your argument, let's do some extra research about the topic. Read the personal experiences about advertising directed at children.

The following is part of an interview about television for a school project by Jimmy Kang.

Q: *How often do you usually watch television?*
Jimmy: I usually watch TV for about one hour a day. If I have a lot of homework, I don't watch it at all.

Q: *Do you ever see ads for children's products when you watch TV?*
Jimmy: Of course! All the time. Most of the ads are for toys, such as cars, action figures, dolls, and building block sets. Some of the ads are for video games. Others are for fast-food restaurants like McDonald's.

Q: *Do you think these ads make you want to have these products?*
Jimmy: I would say so. I mean, when I see the ads, I realize that I'm looking at an ad, so I don't feel like they affect me when I watch them. But then I realize that, say a few hours later, I'm thinking about the toys I saw on TV.

Q: *Why do you think children's advertisements are effective?*
Jimmy: My guess is that they make the products look so cool. The ads are short but show a lot of action with loud sound effects and bright colors. They show things like toy dolls moving by themselves and toy guns making huge explosions. And the kids in the ads are always having lots of fun. So that makes me really want to have the products.

Work with a partner and answer the following questions. Phrases have been provided to help you.

1 How much time does Jimmy spend watching television each day?

→ *Jimmy usually spends* _____.

2 What kinds of products does Jimmy see advertised toward children?

→ *Some of the products are* _____.

3 In what way do the advertisements affect Jimmy?

→ *The ads make Jimmy* _____.

4 Why does Jimmy think advertisements are effective tools?

→ *He believes that* _____.

Your Research

Find an article about advertising directed at children from a magazine, newspaper, or academic website. Paste or tape the article in your workbook in the space below.

Paste or Tape Your Research Article Here

Read your article and write four specific examples or pieces of evidence you can use for your debate. Try to include different types of examples, including opinion polls, statistics, academic studies, and general facts.

- _____
- _____
- _____
- _____

Debate Note-Taking

Use this page to take notes about the opposing team's arguments during the debate.

Note-Taking

Peer Evaluation

Read the assessment criteria and objectively evaluate your peers on a scale from 1 to 10.

CRITERIA	Name				
Understands the subject well	/10	/10	/10	/10	/10
Supports opinion with clear logic and examples	/10	/10	/10	/10	/10
Introduces opinions with appropriate connectors (In my view, I agree, For example, etc.)	/10	/10	/10	/10	/10
Uses a variety of vocabulary and expressions	/10	/10	/10	/10	/10
Accurately uses a variety of grammatical structures	/10	/10	/10	/10	/10
Does not monopolize the conversation and lets other people express themselves	/10	/10	/10	/10	/10
Listens attentively and respects other people's opinions	/10	/10	/10	/10	/10
Is able to accept criticism without becoming upset	/10	/10	/10	/10	/10
TOTAL SCORE	/80	/80	/80	/80	/80

Unit 09 Free College Education

Organizing Ideas

Should college education be made free for everybody?

Look at the reading passage in your textbook. List all the supporting arguments both FOR and AGAINST. Then, add the supporting logic and examples for each argument.

FOR	AGAINST
Argument 1	**Argument 1**
Support	**Support**
Argument 2	**Argument 2**
Support	**Support**
Argument 3	**Argument 3**
Support	**Support**

Making Supporting Examples: Statistics

Statistics are facts based on numbers. They are usually created by governments, universities, news organizations, and companies. Statistics often show the number of people, companies, and nations that agree with a certain opinion or policy. To show these numbers, statistics can include percentages, populations, and points. Below are some statistics related to the topic of free college education.

Additional Research

Before starting your argument, let's do some extra research on the topic. Read the statistics about free college education.

Yearly University Tuition Fees Based on Income in the United States			
Parents' Salary	Expected Yearly Tuition Contribution	Parents' Salary	Expected Yearly Tuition Contribution
$30,000[1]	$560	$80,000	$12,583
$35,000	$1,466	$90,000	$16,218
$40,000	$2,361	$100,000[2]	$19,394
$45,000	$3,212	$125,000[3]	$26,995
$50,000	$3,806	$150,000	$35,637
$55,000	$4,824	$200,000	$51,973
$60,000	$5,984	$250,000[4]	$67,787
$70,000	$8,947	$425,000	$120,057

(1) Eligible for tuition assistance at 2-yr public, 4-yr public, 4-yr private, and 4-yr elite colleges
(2) Eligible for tuition assistance at 4-yr public, 4-yr private, and 4-yr elite colleges
(3) Eligible for tuition assistance at 4-yr elite colleges
(4) Not eligible for any tuition assistance

Work with a partner and answer the following questions. Phrases have been provided to help you.

1. How much money would a student whose parents make $40,000 a year have to pay for college each year? $80,000?

   → A student whose parents earn $40,000 would have to pay _____,

   whereas a student whose parents make $80,000 would pay _____.

2. What is the highest salary a student's parents can have to be eligible for tuition assistance at a two-year college?

   → The highest salary they can have is _____.

3. Why do you think the limit for contribution assistance is higher for elite universities?

   → I think the limit is higher because _____.

4. What is the overall message of this chart?

   → The overall message of the this chart is _____.

Your Research

Find an article about free college education from a magazine, newspaper, or academic website. Paste or tape the article in your workbook in the space below.

Paste or Tape Your Research Article Here

Read your article and write four specific examples or pieces of evidence you can use for your debate. Try to include different types of examples, including opinion polls, statistics, academic studies, and general facts.

- _____
- _____
- _____
- _____

Debate Note-Taking

Use this page to take notes about the opposing team's arguments during the debate.

Note-Taking

_____
_____
_____
_____
_____
_____
_____
_____
_____
_____
_____

Peer Evaluation

Read the assessment criteria and objectively evaluate your peers on a scale from 1 to 10.

CRITERIA	Name				
Understands the subject well	/10	/10	/10	/10	/10
Supports opinion with clear logic and examples	/10	/10	/10	/10	/10
Introduces opinions with appropriate connectors (In my view, I agree, For example, etc.)	/10	/10	/10	/10	/10
Uses a variety of vocabulary and expressions	/10	/10	/10	/10	/10
Accurately uses a variety of grammatical structures	/10	/10	/10	/10	/10
Does not monopolize the conversation and lets other people express themselves	/10	/10	/10	/10	/10
Listens attentively and respects other people's opinions	/10	/10	/10	/10	/10
Is able to accept criticism without becoming upset	/10	/10	/10	/10	/10
TOTAL SCORE	/80	/80	/80	/80	/80

Unit 10: Mandatory Military Service

Organizing Ideas

Should countries require their citizens to serve in the military?

Look at the reading passage in your textbook. List all the supporting arguments both FOR and AGAINST. Then, add the supporting logic and examples for each argument.

FOR

Argument 1

_____
_____
_____

Support

_____
_____
_____

Argument 2

_____
_____
_____

Support

_____
_____
_____

Argument 3

_____
_____
_____

Support

_____
_____
_____

AGAINST

Argument 1

_____
_____
_____

Support

_____
_____
_____

Argument 2

_____
_____
_____

Support

_____
_____
_____

Argument 3

_____
_____
_____

Support

_____
_____
_____

Making Supporting Examples: Facts

A fact is something true. For debates, you can use facts that are common knowledge, but you should also try to use more specific, less commonly known facts. The best places to find specific facts are newspaper and magazine articles. In these sources, you can find all of the details of a situation and can read interviews from people related to the story. Below are some facts related to the topic of mandatory military service.

Additional Research

Before starting your argument, let's do some extra research on the topic. Read the facts about mandatory military service.

- Currently, 63 nations in the world have mandatory military service requirements. Of these, nine countries require both men and women to serve in the military. They include Israel, Cuba, Sudan, and North Korea. The majority of countries do not require military conscription. Some countries, such as the United Kingdom, ended their conscription policy. Other nations, including Iceland and Panama, do not have any military forces at all.

- South Korea has one of the longest military service requirements in the world. The minimum draft period is 21 months, but conscripted soldiers in the special services may have to serve up to 36 months.

- One common objection to mandatory military service is that it goes against personal liberty. Many Americans believe that the government does not have the right to tell people how to live their lives. Eventually, the United States eliminated the draft in 1973. However, President Jimmy Carter restarted the Selective Service in 1980. American men between the ages of 18 and 26 can still be drafted into the military in a time of war.

- People also object to military service because of religious reasons. Some countries, such as Sweden, allow conscripts to serve in noncombat roles such as fireman, nurse, or communications specialist.

Work with a partner and answer the following questions. Phrases have been provided to help you.

1. Which countries require both men and women to serve in the military?
   → *The countries are* _____.

2. What is special about South Korea's military service requirements?
   → *They are special because* _____.

3. Are American men still required to serve in the military? Explain.
   → *American men do not have to do military service, but they still must* _____.

4. Do people who object to military service still have to serve their country? Explain.
   → *People who do not want to fight must still* _____.

Your Research

Find an article about mandatory military service from a magazine, newspaper, or academic website. Paste or tape the article in your workbook in the space below.

Paste or Tape Your Research Article Here

Read your article and write four specific examples or pieces of evidence you can use for your debate. Try to include different types of examples, including opinion polls, statistics, academic studies, and general facts.

- _____
- _____
- _____
- _____

Debate Note-Taking

Use this page to take notes about the opposing team's arguments during the debate.

Note-Taking

Peer Evaluation

Read the assessment criteria and objectively evaluate your peers on a scale from 1 to 10.

CRITERIA	Name				
Understands the subject well	/10	/10	/10	/10	/10
Supports opinion with clear logic and examples	/10	/10	/10	/10	/10
Introduces opinions with appropriate connectors (In my view, I agree, For example, etc.)	/10	/10	/10	/10	/10
Uses a variety of vocabulary and expressions	/10	/10	/10	/10	/10
Accurately uses a variety of grammatical structures	/10	/10	/10	/10	/10
Does not monopolize the conversation and lets other people express themselves	/10	/10	/10	/10	/10
Listens attentively and respects other people's opinions	/10	/10	/10	/10	/10
Is able to accept criticism without becoming upset	/10	/10	/10	/10	/10
TOTAL SCORE	/80	/80	/80	/80	/80

Memo

Memo

DEBATE Pro
Book 3

Workbook